Valiant Young Women

Heroines

Bryce D. Gibby

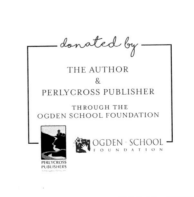

Valiant Young Women, Heroines, 1st Edition.

ATTENTION Universities, Colleges, Churches, Corporations and Professional Organizations: Quantity discounts are available on bulk purchases of this book for educational or gift purposes.

ISBN 0-9741743-1-9

LCCN 2003107215

Published by Perlycross Publishers, 2711 Centerville Road, Suite 120, PMB 5544, Wilmington, Delaware 19808.

Susan G. Hancock, Editor

Cover: Photograph of the statue of the Triumphant Joan of Arc, taken by the author, in the village of Vaucouleurs, France.

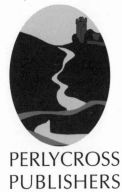

PERLYCROSS
PUBLISHERS
Wilmington, Delaware

"The Perle, as it flows on the north of the Churchyard, the bridge two or three hundred yards below, the vale, and the hills which shape it, are comprised in the perish of Perlycross." R. D. Blackmore

Inspired by Faith

Strength, courage, noble purpose and passions characterize people we hold in high esteem. They inspire us with their assuredness; we even envy the certainty with which they brave the unknown. They gain the status of heroine or hero when they are willing to sacrifice everything to fulfill their life's mission.

Five young heroines are the subjects of Bryce D. Gibby's <u>Valiant Young Women</u>. All teenagers when their missions begin to become apparent to them, each responds to God's calling. Gibby tells us that God has a purpose for everyone that comes into the world and it is each individual's duty and responsibility to ready herself to meet the challenge. We learn about Maria whose uncertain early life, orphaned and cynical, turns into a mountaintop conversion followed by intense religious study. Her marriage and family life as a von Trapp during the Nazi domination of Austria calls on her great faith and bravery to protect her family and the values she holds dear.

We meet Jane Grey who suffered at the hands of a cruel family and was used as a political commodity in the 16th century conflicts over the English throne. Her years of religious study and unshakeable faith meant that she would choose death over renunciation of her beliefs. A similar fate would meet Jeanette of Domremy, Joan d'Arc, who inspired spiritual conversions even as she burned at the stake.

From Irena Gut we learn about the resilience of the human spirit. This young woman, subjected to cruelty, assault and the multiple horrors of a Europe at war not only did what it took to survive but to serve others and live without bitterness at the same time. The admonition to "do what is right" is repeated in the life of Susanna, a devout beauty who lived during the time of the Babylonian captivity. Her virtue is rewarded when her prayers are answered and Daniel appears to defend her and stand for truth.

The author's purpose in presenting these five young lives is to illustrate his belief that true greatness cannot be achieved without the Almighty—that every life is given resources and talents and when used wisely and well, God compounds those resources and the results are marvelous. We are tested through trials and traumas and with each test truth becomes clearer and our spirits grow more steadfast.

Gibby's book offers young readers a notion of heroism that is based on integrity; it offers a portrayal of heroism that is decidedly female showing us that mental and emotional toughness are every bit as critical to greatness as physical toughness often associated with heroes in popular literature. Presented as historical narrative and punctuated with Biblical scripture, the book provides a resource for teachers and other readers who want to explore religious faith and draw moral lessons from some of the world's most engaging personalities.

Whatever the reader's context, <u>Valiant Young Women</u> offers this guidance: The honorable and moral life is a result of deliberate study and reflection and as we come to know the truth, we can and do make right choices. We expect to be tested—life is full of trauma—but it is the source of a richer soul. Know your truth and hear the voice within. Tend to your whole being—body, mind and spirit—and your journey will have meaning and value.

Dr. Brenda L. Bryant, Director
Virginia Women's Institute for Leadership
Mary Baldwin College

Acknowledgements

Of all the heroines in this book only one is still living—Irene Gut Opdyke. Here was a woman of extraordinary faith and courage who ranked equally with the valiant young women of the past of whom I was writing. When I study the lives of historical heroes and heroines I can only imagine what it would be like to actually be in their presence, hear their voice, sense their greatness. Irene, now in her eighties, graciously met with my sister, Susan Hancock, and myself in her modest home in California. Despite her years, Irene is beautiful. She is petite, blonde and delicately featured. Her Polish accent is delightful. She is extremely expressive; the feelings of her heart are clearly made manifest through every feature. As she described to us scenes of pathos, her eyebrows arched high as if to support the burden of memory, her eyes partly closed, moistened and focused on distant visions of great suffering, her shoulders and arms curved inward as if in embrace and her hands clasped tightly to her bosom. Then as if a sudden storm broke forth and in an instant changed the solemn face of the sky from quietude to tempest; her eyes would flash as thunderbolts, her jaw would tighten with indomitable determination, and she would speak with breathtaking fortitude. So here was the young woman who daily risked her life to save life and successfully defied Rokita, the infamous SS Commander. I thank Irene for the profound affect she has had on my life and the commensurate effect upon this work.

I also acknowledge the influence of other women of excellence, for their encouragement and inspiration. I thank my sister, Susan Hancock, for the many hours she spent proof-reading this manuscript and her frank comments, contributions and criticisms. I am grateful to Sharon Thompson and others who sincerely helped me to believe that this type of work is not only desperately needed in our time, but would be accepted by many. Finally, words cannot speak my appreciation towards another woman, a true heroine, who forever will be young, vital and exemplary— who has influenced my life and any work of mine that is in the least measure good—my dear mother, Blanche Slater Gibby.

Contents

Illustrations and Photos Follow Page 88

Preface

The subtitle of this book is simply Heroines. Heroine defined is a female of courage, often of divine ancestry, favored and inspired by the gods, willing to sacrifice all—even life itself—to accomplish a notable purpose. Certainly this denotes that she is heaven sent. Today's contemporary language has been corrupted and we violate the word heroine when we commonly use it to describe the principal female character in a movie or novel—even if she is dissipated, weak willed or governed by carnal passion. We all tend to emulate those whom we regard as heroes or heroines, but this is especially true of young women. We see it in their fashion, speech, and mannerisms. Far more serious than these outward imitations is the insidious adoption by young women of the values of so-called celebrities. More than ever today, young women need to be exposed to the lives of empyrean role models. The narratives of the valiant young women found within these pages are true life stories of real Heroines, young women of profound faith and heroic accomplishment. In a concise manner this book examines the extraordinary lives of Maria Von Trapp, the Lady Jane Grey, Irene Gut, Susanna the Hebrew and Joan of Arc.

This book is not about a particular denomination or a particular genre of religion. One heroine is a Protestant, the next a Catholic, another a Hebrew. There is a God in Heaven who is Father to all the peoples of the earth. He grants light and truth to each person, society and nation according to their own desires to know and live truth. If they live that truth which they have received and in faith recognize Him as the Source of the truth they possess, God blesses them. These blessings come in the form of knowledge and increased power to do good. The more knowledge and wisdom we obtain by faith and diligence, the more knowledge and wisdom we are given; the more good we do, the more good we are able to do. We were designed to have ever increasing intelligence and ability.

The sphere of our influence is also designed to grow. Our first influence is over self. As we exercise authority over our own thoughts, through diligent study and meditation, we receive from God the energy and substance to influence others in ever widening circles. We, in fact, gather the raw materials from God. These are things we have not power to make, but organize them through our efforts of creativity into gifts that we give our fellowman. The more God sees that we rightly use the elements he gives us (whether they are physical, intellectual or spiritual) the more raw materials he makes available to us. Thus the more we possess of His goodness the more good we can give—and so the cycle continues.

At one time each of us left our Father in Heaven's presence with a mission to accomplish on earth, each to be born in a certain age or time, in a certain setting—cultural, political and religious. Some would be born in times and places with great advantage where truth and enlightenment would be easily available. Where much is given, God our Father, expects much. However, many others would be born in times of truth-void famines—times where it would be not only hard to obtain truth, but even extremely dangerous to seek it. Within the limitations of the individual setting in which each soul lives, a merciful Father adapts their life's mission accordingly. There have been great people in history who have been called of God to break limits and found new movements. Others have fulfilled their life's purpose by working within the limitations of their era to accomplish some great good. Joan of Arc was not called to reform Catholicism but to reform France. And God, the giver of her mission, worked within her framework of belief—of truths which she had learned and truths which were available for her to learn. Joan's life and successful completion of her life's mission is awe inspiring and one need not be Catholic to appreciate how faithfully she internalized that light and truth which she received from Heaven and the miraculous good she was able to diligently accomplish.

In all times, ancient, medieval and modern, there have been only two kinds of people on this earth: one looks for answers and guidance horizontally, the other vertically. The first looks earthward, the second looks towards heaven. The first says that seeing is believing. The second knows that believing is seeing. The first believes in nothing that cannot be proven by the five senses. The second knows that there is a sixth sense that works in harmony with the five senses but supercedes them all. This sense is felt in the heart, heard softly in the mind, impressed upon the soul. Heroines possess a profound sixth sense.

Gusti, Child of the Mountains

"When you are a child of the mountains yourself, you really belong to them. You need them. They become the faithful guardians of your life. If you cannot dwell on their lofty heights, if you are in trouble, you want to at least look at them. The man who wrote three thousand years ago: 'I will lift up mine eyes unto the hills, from whence cometh my help,' knew this too. And even Our Lord, when He was weary . . . and wanted to be with His Father, ascended a mountain." — *Maria*

Nestled between the Salzach River and the Gaisberg mountains in Austria rests the arcadian village of Aigen. It is a hamlet of picturesque beauty, of small chalets bordered by rose gardens, verdant meadows waist deep in grass, fertile farmland, lolling cows and stately villas, witnesses of centuries. In the heart of Aigen is a thousand year old inn, the Doktorwirt Hotel. Originally it was a farmhouse, belonging to the estate of a baron and just across the field from his Schloss, or Castle. The Castle still stands in excellent condition, as does this country manor. In the year 1670 the farm house became an inn, later one of the rooms was converted to an icehouse and in recent times the icehouse evolved into a restaurant. Today if you visit this most beautiful hotel you will be greeted by a member of the Karl Schnöll family, owners of the Doktorwirt for five generations. The front desk is managed by the lovely Caroline, dressed in her dirndl, a charming traditional Austrian costume. In the kitchen you will find her brother Karle, a gourmet chef. All of the men of Doktowirt have owned the name Karl. In Austrian an "e" is added to a name to denote "small," or "son of." Working alongside Karle is Elizabeth, twin sister of Caroline. Aunt Lizzie graciously supervises the breakfast area, comprised of a few tables in a wide hallway, and others on the flowered terrace outside. The Doktorwirt is an Austrian Chalet with thick massive walls and a slate roof. Below many of the windows are planter boxes blooming with geraniums and delicate star flowers. Still set in the country, although not far from the city of Salzburg, the hotel is a peaceful haven for the weary traveler. On a June morning the air is melodious with the sounds of church bells and songbirds, and fresh with the scent of newly mowed hay. In the courtyard flagstone steps lead to a sunken lawn edged in ivy. Between the two levels of the terrace is an L-shaped flower garden, a veritable collage of color—azaleas, roses, sweet williams, peonies, phlox, iris and pansies, intermixed with sweet smelling herbs.

Gazing upon this idyllic setting with its wild flower meadows, its rolling green mountains to the east and the towering granite peaks of the Alps to the west, it is hard to imagine that this peace could ever be disturbed.

"Beautiful, isn't it?"

Aunt Lizzy is speaking and at her side is Caroline. Her kind eyes smile at their corners.

"I remember when I was just a little girl and my brother Karl was a small boy of four. He would go to the fourth floor windows and yell, 'Achtung, Achtung! The bombers are coming.' Then he would throw all of our pillows out the window and 'bomb' us who were standing below."

She laughs at the memory, while Caroline laughs heartily with her. They are a contented happy family who deeply appreciate the blessings of serenity. Her eyes become more serious and reflective.

"Mamma didn't like his game and she would gather all of the pillows off the ground and would scold him a little. Of course he was playing out a terrible reality. Towards the end of the war we would hear the bombers coming. A distant drone at first, then growing louder and louder. I can still hear it in my mind."

She makes the sound of the aircraft engines and her eyes look skyward.

"We would run to a place we called the 'witches hole,' a cave in the ground where we used to play. There we would find many of our neighbors who lived closer to this natural shelter. Then we would hear the deafening explosions of the bombs and feel the ground shake around us. When the sounds would stop we would climb out and look at the massive craters blown in the fields there (and she points to meadows to the east and south). One bomb grazed our home over there (and she points to the northeast wall). You see the allies knew that Heinrich Himmler lived here in Aigen and they were trying to blow up his home. He lived just across this field. But they never hit it. Mostly all they hit were open fields."

The Nazi SS chief Himmler had confiscated the most beautiful mansion in this pastoral region to use as his residence and headquarters from 1940 until Germany's defeat in 1945. This home also still stands. It was built in 1860 and was known as the Villa vol Burga. An exquisite example of Austrian architecture, it is to this day a palatial jewel. The estate of 33,000 square meters is enclosed by a stone fence finished with stucco, built at the command of Himmler. The forced laborers who erected the wall were summarily executed, murdered, when the wall was completed.

She stood alone on the glacial mountain, slowly winding the rope into a coil. All of her friends had descended to the camp below. The sky was crimson and the sun so low that alpine peaks cast giant shadows across the ice fields. The dying day, more brilliant and dynamic in its last moments, deeply moved her soul. The contrast between light and shade is greatest just before sunset. Valleys are etched in ebony. Back-lit summits, when viewed at close range, are well defined profiles. That which is still illumined greets the eye arrayed in color. In mid day, the harsh light of the sun at its zenith overpowers color, narrowing the spectrum. But that light which precedes twilight allows our eyes to see infinite hues, broad wavelengths of harmonizing chroma. This moment of revelation is lost the instant the sun descends below the horizon and the curtain of dusk falls. One must really *see* when it is time to see, before nightfall obliterates vision. And one cannot go down before the sun does to rest at the camp in the shadows of the mountains and experience transcendental sight.

Of all the graduating students who had gone to the high Alps on a weeklong excursion, only Maria remained on the crest of the glacier. Their guide trusted Maria, who was experienced in mountain climbing, to be the last off the summit. She was far from the towns of Tirol—removed even from the laughter of her classmates. She gazed intently upon the splendor of the clarion light that rested as the fire of Pentecost upon the granite peaks. Her heart must have felt the same sentiments that caused Ezekiel to write:

And the glory of the LORD went up from the midst of the city, and stood upon the mountain . . . [And he heard the voice of the Lord say] I will put a new spirit within you; and I will take the stony heart out . . .

3

Only a few weeks earlier Maria had been agnostic, if not atheistic. Her life had been so difficult as a child that her heart and spirit were in danger of petrifaction. But that was before she had met Father Kronseder. In one evening he had touched her with such love that she had begun to understand, once again, the love of God. Now, upon her Mount Sinai, as she viewed the majesty of creation, she was being re-created by the Almighty. First she was overcome with appreciation—then with the desire to sacrifice and serve.

Praying aloud, Maria asked Heavenly Father what she could give back to Him for the wonderful creation He had given her. What would be the greatest gift she could ever give? Then suddenly one thought surfaced: the best gift is what we love best.

Right there and then Maria decided to give her life to God. She hurried down the slope and said goodbye to her friends. She was so anxious to begin her quest that she could not wait until morning but made her way, alone, off the mountain. Then she ran to a village train station, boarded the next train to Salzburg and arrived in that beautiful city at 6:30 a.m. Maria asked a policeman at the railroad station, "Sir, could you please tell me which is the strictest convent in this town?"

Maria's father had been married twice and twice had become a widower. His first wife was killed when their horse drawn buggy met with disaster on a narrow bridge spanning a wild mountain waterfall. They were both thrown over the rail but the young wife was swept over the falls and drowned. Brokenhearted, he gave his infant son to the care of a matronly cousin in Vienna and left Austria. For a number of years he traveled the globe, monetarily supporting his son, but never fathering him. When he finally returned home, his son had grown into a man, a complete stranger to him.

Not long after his return to Vienna he met Maria's mother who was only eighteen years of age. Incredibly she bore an amazing resemblance to his first wife. They were married soon after and it wasn't long before the young bride was expecting her first child. Indicative of her impetuous nature, Maria was born on a *train*. Her mother was returning to Vienna from a Christmas holiday in Tirol when she went into labor. So eager was the infant Maria to begin the adventure of life that she just would not wait a few hours more to be born in the General Hospital in Vienna. Having entered mortality traveling she would prove to be a traveler all the days of her life.

Sadly, for this new family, their promise of happiness was not to be. When Maria was three years of age her mother contracted pneumonia. Without the aid of antibiotics she was beyond the aid of doctors. Her father believed that if he held his beloved upright, she would not die. And so Maria's mother left this life in his arms, held lovingly against his heart.

Now, like so many years before, her father was alone with a tiny child. Again, he carried his toddler to the same loyal cousin. Like her brother, Maria would be raised—not by her mother, but by a woman willing to mother.

In her foster home Maria was the only child. It was a household of adults. Her foster parents lived with their four grown up children—Alfred, Pepi, Anni and Kathy. They were all set in their ways and did not allow other children to visit or play with Maria. She was dropped off at school and picked up the moment school let out so she did not have the opportunity of even walking to and from school with girlfriends.

Without playmates her life was very lonely. But her spirit was indomitable—if she could not have a loving family and kind friends in reality, she could in her imagination. And so she pretended that she lived with a large family named Paultraxi. She invented every detail of a happy life—they lived on a beautiful farm, were very jolly and freely hugged and kissed each other. They had lots of interesting visitors who were always kind to each other and to her, and always happy. When Maria's foster family was away from home, she loved dragging all the chairs from every room and grouping them in a large circle. Then she would spend her solitary time entertaining her imaginary family. She served them exquisite refreshments and carried on lively conversations. Though her foster mother was kind, she was very practical and when she happened upon this disruption in her household, she soundly scolded Maria for such fancies.

Although her foster mother did not understand her need for companionship, friends, and a normal childhood, still she was sincerely religious and would take Maria with her to church every morning. There were special moments when she would hold Maria on her lap and show her the pictures in her illustrated Bible. One time Maria demonstrated what came to be her characteristic spunk. When she saw a picture of Christ being tormented she grabbed a crochet hook and pierced the eyes out of "those bad men torturing our dear Lord." Her foster mother taught her fundamental truths that Maria truly believed when she was little and later returned to when she graduated from high school. She was taught that it is impossible to hide from God, that he sees everything you do. She was taught and felt the love of God, that he is truly a kind Heavenly Father, who takes great joy in our goodness and is "very sad when we are bad." She also was taught to pray. When Maria was in the third grade she made her first communion, beautifully dressed in white. Her desire was to never offend God and belong to him all the days of her life.

During these years Maria's father visited her—sometimes at her foster-home in Kagran. At other times he would take her to his large apartment in Vienna. He did not call her Maria, but "Gusti," her deceased mother's name. Mostly she enjoyed these visits for her father was a very interesting man. He had returned to Austria a linguist, speaking fourteen languages. He had collected living birds from the four corners of the earth and had created an amazing aviary right in the apartment. It was a wonderland, an interior island of exotic birds, some small and some quite large, of every color and description—chirping, singing, contentedly fluttering about, filling Maria with happiness and her father with pride.

He was also an accomplished musician possessing an incredible assortment of instruments in the families of brass, viol, and flute. He entertained Maria playing melodies from far off places. But alas, with all of his gifts he was not a teacher. He would briefly demonstrate how an instrument was to be played and expect immediate results. His disappointment in her early attempts, and his perpetual impatience with what was actually a gifted child's ability, often reduced little Maria to tears. At times he took her traveling with him. But he had never learned fathering or nurturing skills and could not relate to his child, and these trips were never enjoyable for her. Maria wished her father could have lived to see her develop her musical talents and her love for travel and adventure. As peers, they would have had much in common.

A nine year old when her father died, Maria had been a submissive and obedient little girl. Her natural inclination was to please the small circle of adults that made up her family. Her foster mother scolded her if she misbehaved and she accepted such correction with resolve to improve, as a good child would. As a fifth grader she was given greater freedoms—such as walking to and from school with girls her own age. She loved this liberty and with her newfound friends would window shop in the village or play games along the walkway. But when her father's life ended so did these happy days. Her foster mother's oldest daughter had recently married a judge—a rigid, neurotic, disciplinarian. This man, known to her as Uncle Franz, assumed her guardianship. He decreed that she must come straight home from school with "no fooling around." Like a Nazi interrogator, he frightened her, telling her that she could hide nothing from him, that he "had his ways of finding out everything."

It didn't matter how hard she tried to please him or how swiftly she hurried home from school—Maria was greeted with beatings. If she remonstrated her innocence she was slapped hard across the face and called a liar. At first she lived in habitual fear of her step-uncle Franz. But the effect of the beatings took an unexpected turn. Instead of forcing her to cower more deeply to this insane tormentor (for he was mad and was later committed to an asylum where he ultimately died), the abuse toughened her.

In her twelfth year she realized that she could take whatever he dished out. No longer afraid, and knowing she would be harshly punished for good behavior as well as for misbehavior, she resolved to strike back in the only way she could—she would in fact do the very things he accused her of doing. Maria started a new life. Defiantly, she skipped school, spent time with her friends, bought pastries with her school money and changed from a fearful, timid child to an outgoing, gregarious, social individual. Frequently she came home very late, knowing her impending punishment, yet taking inward pleasure in "having lived."

For Step-uncle Franz, Maria felt only bitter contempt. For years she had innocently suffered his brutality and now she resolved that she would never again answer him truthfully . . . never. This was a time of paradox for Maria. While on the one hand she acted in direct opposition to Uncle Franz, on the other hand she adopted his passion for the new socialist regime and its anti-religious dogma. Atheism was a course he served and she devoured at every meal. Her beloved biblical stories from her early childhood were mocked as feebleminded superstitions.

However, Maria's ties to her Heavenly Father were stronger than she then realized—for she was drawn inexorably to the peace of His creation. When she cut class, as an act of rebellion against her guardian, she escaped, not to the society of gangs of delinquents, but rather she fled to the refuge of "wheat fields" and "woodlands." She loved to gather wild flowers and loaded her arms with them. Without regard to the consequences she would return home and arrange lovely bouquets, filling their house with beauty, a soft contrast to her Uncle's severity. This of course was also a defiant display that she had skipped class.

Fortunately her bright mind and ability to cram for exams got her through school despite these aberrant escapades. Needless to say, her disregard for proper demeanor and flippant attitude made her popular with a certain crowd at school, but not with her instructors. She was their "horror and fright." Punishment from teachers was mild in comparison to the abuse at home; thus Maria feared nothing and reveled in mischief. At age fourteen, during her last year at school, one instructor confronted her before the class, "I wish on you a daughter exactly like yourself."

Interestingly enough Maria loved to learn and set her sights upon the State Teacher's College of Progressive Education. But higher education required money that Maria did not have. Certainly her father had left an estate but she was too naive to ask her step-uncle for her inheritance. Fortunately however, her spirit of self-reliance was growing ever stronger and she formulated a courageous plan of independence. A friendship had been forged between Maria and a fellow classmate, Annie, a girl who spent her summers with her mother in the resort village of Semmering. Three days after graduation Maria deposited her meager belongings into a large straw suitcase, kissed her old foster-mother goodbye, stole quietly into Uncle Franz's bedroom and while he slept, relieved him of his pocket money which lay upon his night stand. She ran as fast as she could to South Railroad Station and purchased a third class ticket for Semmering. Annie's widowed mother, a laundress, graciously received Maria into her small home and family of eight. It is interesting how those with so little often share the most.

Early the next morning Maria set out to apply for work at all twenty-eight hotels in town. At fourteen, Maria was tall, very thin and wore her long hair in two braids which hung to her knees. It is not surprising that her applications as a tutor for vacationing children were all declined. As she canvassed the twenty-eight hotels a second time, she vowed to do any job, but was again refused. The following day, however, the manager of the largest hotel in the town offered Maria the position as umpire of their tennis tournament. His regular umpire had become ill, the tournament was beginning that very afternoon, and he was desperate for someone who knew the game. She had never heard of tennis before, and did not know if one played it with feet or hands. Cleverly, she looked at him and asked which rules would be used here. Instantly, a detailed explanation was supplied. Maria was a quick study and a natural actress, having learned from the Hotel manager exactly how the game was played, she immediately began her summer career as a sports official.

All week long Maria sat high upon her umpire seat calling plays and was paid a fantastic sum for her services. By the summer's end she had earned a considerable amount of money, and that coupled with high marks on her entrance exam qualified her for a scholarship, and made it possible for her to enter the State Teachers' College in September.

As most young people discover, college is very different from secondary school. For Maria it was especially wonderful—without assistance from Uncle Franz she had earned this opportunity. She was on her own and she loved the liberty. Maria discovered that she not only loved to learn, but also she loved to teach. She entered into a program of self-reformation, vowing to be "passionately truthful" and dedicated herself to her studies. But not all of Uncle Franz's fetters could be easily shaken off. A natural leader, she soon found she attracted a following and unfortunately began to convert them to her atheistic way of thinking. She would tell her friends that it was ludicrous to lean upon religion with all of its impractical symbols, its sacraments, effigies, books of prayer, and old Bible. She told them they could prove to the Catholics that they could excel without "crutches" as long as they worked hard and were determined. Her humanistic arguments won to her side a majority:

"trying to prove to ourselves and everybody else that a decent life can be lived without God."

The power of *one* is amazing, for either good or ill. Hitler was just one, yet this solitary, coarse, Luciferic despot thrust the entire world into war and was personally responsible for the murders of millions. Gandhi was just one, yet without bloodshed he was personally responsible for the liberation of a nation, freeing millions. Maria was soon to meet one person who, in a moment's time, changed her life forever. He would do this by helping her to understand the love of that One individual on whom all else depends.

When not at her studies, Maria was involved in three other activities. She had many expenses that were not covered by her scholarship and so she did embroidery work for the Quaker's Society of Friends, being paid "by the inch." This was the time of the famine in Vienna and the Society also provided every student with one hot meal a day. Maria said that if it had not been for this she might have literally starved. Secondly, she loved to hike the glorious Alps and with her schoolmates would cover tremendous distances on foot; thirdly, she had inherited from her natural father a great love of music. As often as possible she attended Mass, not for any religious benefit, of course. She hated to even think that anyone might mistake her motivation, but Mass enabled her to hear the compositions of the masters performed by some of the greatest choirs on earth.

It was on Palm Sunday in the last year of college that she saw crowds of people entering a large cathedral in Vienna and surmised that they must be going to hear the *St. Matthew Passion* by Bach. But instead of Bach they were assembled to hear the famous Father Kronseder. Maria was amazed! Instead of being repulsed by his sermon, the customary reaction induced by her stepfather Franz, she was entirely overwhelmed by his discourse on the atonement of Jesus Christ. Afterwards, she worked her way through the maze of people to the pulpit. As Father Kronseder came near her, Maria loudly asked him if he actually believed what he had preached. His answer was brief, "Don't you?" Maria said that of course she did not! In a condescending manner she explained that she attended the State Teachers College of Progressive Education, a well-known socialist institution.

Father Kronseder did not engage Maria in a discussion right there and then, as she might have wished, but told her he would see her at a set time and place. Without waiting for her reply he politely excused himself. The meeting time he appointed was right in the middle of a skiing holiday Maria had planned with her friends. Nevertheless, Maria was there, at the church, at the time he had given her. Father Kronseder greeted her warmly and for over two hours non-stop listened to her faithless arguments— those dogmas she had assimilated from Uncle Franz and her socialistic professors at college. During the entire interview, not once did he offer a counter proposition but simply waited until she had completely exhausted her position. When at length she was silent, Father Kronseder calmly said, "Well, my dear, you simply have been wrongly informed." With that he gave her a reading assignment.

It is an interesting fact that most people, when they begin to study the writings of the faith-critics, the scoffers, the anti-religionists—those who under various names and feigned purposes, seek to destroy faith and replace it with nothingness—it is interesting that they give countless hours to reading these nihilists and yet give no time to the serious study of the scriptures, no time to sincere prayer, no time to true service, no time to the study of the inspired writings of God-knowing men and women. Thus they acquire only doubts, unresolved conflicts, theories, skepticism and fears. Their only confidence is in their feeble and faulted sight, that which is "proven" today, only to be disproved tomorrow. Having never invested in real faith, and the wealth of knowledge that God has directly revealed to his eye-witnesses, the prophets, and the vast body of evidence found in inspired texts, in the heavens above and the earth beneath, they are left spiritually void—empty cisterns.

Across the border from Maria's native Tirol, in the Bavarian Alps, stands the most beautiful castle in the world, Neuschwanstein—translated in English, *New Swan Stone*. Its symmetry, grace, romantic style, and setting approach architectural perfection. King Ludwig II devoted his life and his royal treasury, employing the craftsman, artisans, and citizens of his provinces in its creation, in building a celestial palace, not to honor himself, but the true King of Kings. Regarding this structure Ludwig wrote to a dear friend:

> "It is my intention to have the old castle ruin of Hohenschwangau . . . built anew in the true style of Germany's old knights' castles . . . a number of guest rooms are to be appointed in a homely and comfortable manner; you know the name of the revered Guest I hope to lodge there; the place is one of the finest to be found, sacred and unapproachable, a worthy temple for the divine Friend through whom the world's only salvation and true blessing came into blossom."

There were others in King Ludwig's age who spent their energies refining and advancing the design of the trebuchet, catapults of great power. The medieval trebuchet made it possible to hurl stones of tremendous weight. Later these engineers of war became cable of projecting heavy fire balls of iron through the air; and now finally they have achieved the capability of hurling their missiles across continents and oceans. The purpose of the trebuchet is singular—destruction.

We can really only do one thing at a time. We can either acquire the knowledge to build castles or catapults. We can either create or destroy. For years Maria had been hurling stones against the faith of others, now she desired to build a new life, a "worthy temple for the divine Friend." She put her whole being into her new studies. She was amazed to read well supported arguments of faith and while she read, she gratefully acknowledged the spiritual confirmation she felt within her soul. Her intellect quickly registered the "non emotional, cold facts which were the absolute opposite of what I had learned from my uncle and school teachers," while her tender heart, through the kindness of Father Kronseden, felt the "genuine love," the "true compassion" and sacrifice of her Lord for her.

She came to this knowledge with an awakening of the harm she had done to the faith of her associates. With only a few weeks remaining before graduation, Maria began her own crusade—working desperately to rekindle the convictions of religious truth within the hearts of all of her friends whom she had led astray. Her conscience was her guide. By following the impressions of the Spirit she proved to be an effective missionary, reclaiming to God all but one—and as the Lord often recalls to our minds that which we have previously been taught, who knows but what that one "lost soul" ultimately was persuaded aright by Maria's zeal.

When Maria had left home four years earlier to escape the brutality of her Uncle Franz, her old foster-mother, knowing that Maria had come to accept the atheism of her son-in-law, held her face, kissed her gently, and vowed to pray every day for Maria. She told Maria that she knew that all would be well with her, that her faith would return. Her mother's prayers had been answered. After graduation from college, Maria declared: "Once again God was back in my life." And so it was that Maria had descended from the white-capped mountains having promised God that her life was now His to mold.

Overlooking Salzburg stands the medieval Fortress Hohensalzburg. The first fortifications were erected by Romans. Over the centuries its walls grew incredibly high with massive ramparts. The citadel was never taken in battle. This white-stoned superstructure retains its prominence, towering above the city that kneels, as it were, at its feet, as far away as Aigen. Just below the great walls of Hohensalzburg, at the southern extremity, but still elevated above the Altstadt (historic city) is the

Benedictine Abby of Nonnberg. Nonnberg was established in the year 700 by Saint Rupert for his sister, as a community of nuns dedicated to an austere and strict order.

It was to this Abby that Maria applied on that fateful summer's morning. Considering the manner in which she presented herself it is a wonder that she was accepted! There Maria stood in full hiking regalia, complete with ice pick, coiled ropes, knapsack, and bronze skin from her days in the sun. The interviewing nun, perhaps startled by this unorthodox youth, asked if someone had sent Maria. To this Maria laughed and with characteristic pluck answered that she had never yet obeyed anyone and if someone had told her to come, she would not have done it.

Amid looks of unbelief and raised eyebrows, Maria was admitted into the convent by the Reverend Mother Abbess. The Abbess must have perceived that beyond this animated tom-boy personality was the potential for greatness. As it soon became apparent that Maria did not fit in the novitiate, a private Mistress of Novices was assigned to her for she must learn to become a girl before she could ever become a nun. Although filled with goodwill Maria's free spirit just could not be contained, and as a result, she was in continual trouble. Her first impulse when meeting a barrier was to create some way around it; and she applied this technique with the rules of the Abby, such as whistling. She reasoned that the basis of the rule against whistling was to prevent the intrusion of worldly music; so Maria whistled classical works or hymns. She slid down banisters, jumped over chimneys, leaped up and down stairs several at a time; such things were no feat for one who had scaled the Alps. A postulant should never correct a superior nun, the penalty was to repent by kissing the floor. Maria was full of ideas and suggestions, having just graduated from a teaching institution. So when she saw her head mistress coming, she proceeded to kneel, kiss the floor, and then say exactly what she had on her mind.

There was so much for Maria to learn in these two years at Nonnberg. Her days began at 5:00 a.m., not to go hiking as in former days, but to pray for an hour and a half, spend most of the day in deep silence, and assist in the daily mass. And there were set punishments for mishaps and misbehavior. However, this chastisement was nothing like the brutality she had received at the hand of her Uncle Franz. For example when she broke something, which happened frequently, she had to bring the item with her to the next meal and say:

> "I, the most unworthy member of this holy community, have wasted common good."

Then she had to show the broken object to the group and then lie down upon the stone floor. She remained there during the meal until she heard a gentle tap on the table. Upon hearing this tap she was allowed to rise and receive whatever courses of the meal that had not yet been served. It was not uncommon for Maria to miss a good part of the repast and sometimes the entire meal!

Those precious years were not all difficulty and punishment. Nonnberg shaped and balanced Maria's life, for which she was very grateful. The ascetic life at the Abby did not chafe her buoyancy—she needed and loved it! Nonnberg truly became home where Maria learned discipline. Her uncle's cruelty had only taught her disobedience. Now Maria knew what it meant to control her own stubborn will, to curb her tongue and to obey without always knowing why. Over the next two years she thrived in the warm atmosphere of love and security within the ancient walls of Nonnberg Abby. For the first time, she knew what it meant to be loved and, as a result, her character blossomed.

Maria became a fifth grade teacher who loved her students as if they were her own children. She so much enjoyed taking her class outdoors, sitting with them on the ground and telling them stories, or playing with them. And how she loved to teach them to sing! Her manner of teaching excited some concern in the old-fashioned Nonnberg—but the superintendent of schools, after visiting Maria's classroom, congratulated the Reverend Mother for having such an outstanding teacher!

Then came the day when Maria was "loaned" by the Reverend Mother to Baron von Trapp. The true account of this loosely follows the story portrayed in the movie *The Sound of Music*. Two inscriptions at Nonnberg became the motif for Maria's life. In the cell where she slept, painted in old-fashioned letters above the door the first inscription read: *Thy will be done*. In the centuries old graveyard of Nonnberg the second inscription read: *God's Will Hath No Why*. One day as Maria was correcting her student's papers old Sister Lucia informed her that she was wanted by the Reverend Mother. Immediately Maria's conscience was alarmed. She thought, *Just what does she know?* When at last she reached the Reverend

Mother's room and heard her kind "Ave," which meant for her to enter the chamber, she relaxed and put her fears aside.

The Reverend Mother sat Maria next to her, held both of her hands, looked deep into her eyes and said:

"Tell me, Maria, which is the most important lesson our old Nonnberg has taught you?"

Maria answered without hesitation:

"The only important thing on earth for us is to find out what is the Will of God and to do it."

The Abbess griped her hands even tighter.

"Even if it is not pleasant, or if it is hard, perhaps very hard?"

Maria responded with certainty:

"Yes, Reverend Mother, even then, and wholeheartedly, too."

The stage was set, Reverend Mother then explained to Maria that God's will was for her to leave the Abby for nine months. The doctor felt that Maria's reoccurring headaches were the result of too abrupt a change from her vigorous outdoor life to the quiet sedentary existence at Nonnberg. That very day Baron von Trapp, a retired Naval captain, had requested a teacher for his chronically ill daughter. Maria was assigned to leave that very afternoon for the Villa von Trapp. Though broken hearted at leaving her beloved Abby, Maria resolved, nevertheless, to obey the will of God.

A few hours later, dressed in outdated, ill fitting civilian clothes, Maria descended down the 144 steps from Nonnberg and from the Residenzplatz in Salzburg boarded the bus bound for Aigen. Years earlier the Baron had purchased the Villa vol Burga, the most beautiful estate in the area, and it became the Villa Trapp. In a little less than half an hour she was dropped at the doorway of the ancient inn in Aigen. In the doorway a man stood smoking. When Maria asked him directions to the Villa von Trapp, he stepped out and pointed toward tall distant trees across a green expanse of meadows.

On the other side of the meadow was a park hedged by a nearly solid wall of green bushes and trees. Maria could hardly get a peep of the mansion until she made her way around to the front where a large iron gate marked the entrance to the estate. What she saw may still be seen to this day. Rising from a stately courtyard and framed by lush and lofty hardwood trees stands the Villa Trapp—truly Austrian in character, multi-leveled, massive, splendid! The front elevation has four main reliefs, the third from the right is the grand entrance with three white archways. The center arch curves over two-winged large oaken doors, while the others frame windows set behind chalet style grid-work. At the base of these arches are beautiful planters, blooming in red. Above these archways are three grand Christian windows, their panes set into main supports that form an upright cross. Dormers project from a highly decorative orthodox Austrian roof. The northern division of the mansion is crowned by a tower, which rises into a spire at its summit. The exterior stucco is now pale yellow accented by the white of the archways, green shutters and the steel-gray roof. The overall impression is one of grandeur and grace.

As Maria approached the villa, she could see through the windows that there was something very large hanging inside—it was red and white. At the door was a distinguished looking man. After Maria enthusiastically introduced herself calling him "Captain," he stiffly answered that he was the butler, Hans. Then he ushered Maria into a lofty hall that vaulted to the villas full height. She so much wanted to ask him questions for she had never before met a naval captain. But Hans' manner was very formal and he hastily left her alone, seated on a dark, ornately carved chair. (This chair is one of three pieces, which remain in the Villa to this day.) Looking around, Maria saw three large windows streaming an abundance of sunshine onto an elegant staircase which curved past the red and white wall hanging—it was in fact an enormous Austrian flag nearly thirty feet in length.

As she studied the beautiful flag, she heard energetic footsteps coming toward her. It was the Captain! He was not anything like the "old sea wolf" that Maria had expected. Baron Georg von Trapp was tall and well dressed. He had a manner of self-assurance and as he spoke to Maria, he shook her hand warmly.

Each was astonished by the other; he by her out-dated appearance and she by the brass whistle he pulled from his pocket. Explaining that she must meet his children, the Captain began trilling a musical code which echoed through the house. Unlike Christopher Plummer who portrayed him in the *The Sound of Music*, when it came to his family, Captain von Trapp was a kind and gentle man. The whistle was a practical and dignified solution—not just because there were so many children to call, but their home was so large and their grounds so vast that the only alternative would have been a loud-speaker system. The whistle was used for the same purpose as the dinner bell on an American ranch, but allowed for individual summons. However, the children did form into a sober, silent procession and descended down the great stairway in matching blue sailor suits. Maria was impressed by the polite "little ladies and gentlemen," who hearing the introduction of their father echoed: "*Grüss Gott*, Fräulein Maria."

Captain Georg von Trapp was a retired naval officer—retired in that Austria had lost its seaport in the reshuffling of borders that followed World War I. He was also a war hero. He first distinguished himself in the Boxer Rebellion in China, receiving the Silver Medal of Honor. In the Great War he volunteered his services to command one of the first torpedo-equipped submarines in naval history. This was extremely dangerous duty for the technology then extant was primitive, the submarines slow, cumbersome and plagued with deadly fumes. Nevertheless Captain von Trapp received accolade upon accolade from the Imperial Navy and the Austrian Nation as he stealthy prowled the waters of the Adriatic Sea destroying enemy ships in defense of his homeland. He became respected, not only by his military peers, but by his country who looked upon him as a beloved son, a mighty defender in a crucial time. The highest honor a naval commander could receive was the Cross of Empress Maria Theresien, given only during time of war for a successful "act of personal bravery, performed on one's own initiative at one's own risk, sometimes even against orders." Before the war's end Captain von Trapp was awarded this Cross of the Empress and was given the title of Baron with all of the commensurate honors and privileges. There were those who believed that he would be promoted to the exalted position of Lord Admiral, Commander of the entire Navy. But when the war ended, his country was shorn of her coastline; there was no fleet left to command.

The striking young officer had, in 1912, married a remarkable young lady in her own right—the accomplished Agathe Whitehead. Granddaughter of the inventor of the torpedo and daughter of industrialist Robert Whitehead, she was an heiress of great beauty, grace, and character. The young mother bore him five girls and two boys, ages fourteen to four: Rupert, Agathe, Maria, Werner, Hedwig, Johanna, and Martina. Then disaster struck—in 1922, not long after little Martina was born, Agathe, Georg's beloved wife, died of scarlet fever. Georg had loved the Navy and lost it; now he had lost the love of his life, his cherished companion. Publicly he was a national hero, especially venerated by the youth of Austria, yet privately, stunned by the death of his wife and by the collapse of his naval career, he seemed to loose purpose; life felt hollow—empty.

This in spite of his great paternal affection, for Georg loved his children with all of his conscious heart. However, so much of his heart was somnolent and needed to be awakened. It was expected that he would remarry a true princess—the lovely Princess Yvonne. How Maria hoped and prayed that Yvonne would be a good mother—for in an instant Maria had fallen in love, not with the Baron, but with his dear children.

She had been sent to tutor sick little Maria, who had contracted scarlet fever at the time of her mother's death. During and after their lessons, the other children began drifting in; for they were drawn to Maria like a magnet. They were starved for feminine affection, often wrapping their little arms around her neck and covering her face with kisses. It was literally the first time in her life that she experienced this type of affection. In the evenings Maria and the children gathered before a warm fire. The little ones climbed into Maria's lap while the others snuggled next to her on the floor. She told them stories and they responded with pure unrestrained affection. Maria folded all of them in her arms and called this, her "own true love story."

Our lives missions interweave, like harmonizing threads of different hues in a grand tapestry. One heroine is called to bear seven wondrous children—to carry their tiny growing bodies until, through her agonizing travail, they miraculously enter mortal life. Then beyond all human understanding she suffers death, leaving a desperate bereaved husband and more heartrending still, seven sad motherless children. Another heroine is called as a *helpmate* to a good man, to awaken the benumbed recesses of his heart, to love and nurture that which is most dear and precious to him. It is heroic for any woman to unselfishly bring life into this world, but still more so to accept the responsibility and mission of rearing that issue which is not her own, yet loving them as if they were, and that at the tender age of twenty—a scarce six years older than the oldest child. Maria would be the last in a long line of twenty-six nurses, governesses and teachers to care for the von Trapp family.

Whatever affection Georg had for Princess Yvonne vanished as he observed the young, vivacious and magical Maria work and play with his children. How she loved them; and how, therefore, could he keep from loving her? Yvonne desired a non-cumbersome life with Georg, a life of adult sociality in the regal circles to which they both belonged. After their marriage it was the Princess's plan to conveniently board the children aristocratically at private schools. While Maria, with no aspirations of becoming a baroness—for she was still determined to serve her Lord as a nun, had spliced her life's threads to those wonderful fibers of their natural mother.

How did Maria regard Georg? Through the passing months, between frequent business and hunting trips, the Captain joined in with the activities of Maria and his children. When they played volleyball, he joined in; when they hiked the mountains near their home, he came along; in the evenings when they gathered before the fire, Maria played her guitar and the Captain surprised them by pulling out his long unused violin to join them in music and laughter. Maria *liked* the Captain, however her focus was still upon what she thought would be her life's mission. As long as she was anxiously anticipating the day when she would take the vows of a nun there was virtually no room in her heart for feelings of romance.

Twelve days before Maria was scheduled to leave the Villa von Trapp and return to Nonnberg the three youngest von Trapp children ran in to Maria, who was busy cleaning a chandelier. The Baron had recently returned from visiting Princess Yvonne where he had broken his engagement, telling her that he was in love with someone else. He had kept himself sequestered in his study and had not discussed the recent turn of events with anyone. Now with the children at her feet, Maria, intent on cleaning, heard them prattle something about their father wondering if she even liked him. Maria continued working, answering vaguely that, of course, she liked the Captain. They clattered off.

Later that night Georg watched Maria arrange a vase of peonies. In a warm voice he thanked her for what she had said, telling her that it was so very nice of her. Maria looked up wondering what he could possibly be referring to. As she met his eyes, his intent look, so loving and full of gratitude, confused and bewildered her. She lowered her eyes instantly and asked him hesitantly what it was that she had said. Now it was Georg's turn to be surprised and he questioned her, saying:

"Why, didn't you send word to me through the children that you accepted the offer, I mean, that you want to marry me?"

Maria was so startled that her flowers and scissors fell in a heap on the floor. She stammered:

"Marry you?"

"Well, yes. The children came to me this morning and said they had had a council among themselves, and the only way to keep you with us would be that I marry you. I said to them that I would love to, but I didn't think you liked me. They ran over to you and came back in a flash, crying that you had said, 'yes I do.' Aren't we engaged now?"

Certainly Maria's reaction disappointed the Captain but he was absolutely dismayed when Maria explained that she still planned to enter the convent and take her vows as a nun. All along Maria had held fast that she was only *loaned* from Nonnberg—but now there was more to consider. How she loved the children and this highly unorthodox proposal centered on their needs. Had Maria been approached in any other way she would certainly have flatly refused. But the sad look in Georg's eyes and the gentle tug of those maternal tendrils that were winding round her heart would not allow her to refuse him unconditionally. Yet this was above her—Maria was so young and felt so many conflicting emotions. Hadn't she promised God that she would give her life to him? She loved Nonnberg and the simple life of service that would there be hers. She also loved the von Trapp children and knew how badly they needed a good mother. Hadn't she prayed to her Father in Heaven that He would send them a wonderful mother who would care for them as if they were her own? Was she being sent in answer to her own prayer? It is one thing to see the very real needs of others and ask God to bless them. It is quite another thing to recognize the fact, that having perceived the need we have a responsibility to give whatever relief and aid is in our power to grant— so the parable of the *Good Samaritan* teaches. Maria responded that she would counsel with the Reverend Mother at Nonnberg—that she wanted to do the will of God and had faith that Heavenly Father would use this good woman as his instrument to reveal to her what His will was concerning this crucial decision.

Maria immediately set out for the Abby. The Reverend Mother acknowledged that this was the most important decision of her life. She then assembled "the community" to ask God what was His will in the matter. They prayed and counseled together and then the Reverend Mother returned to the humble Maria, who was still on her knees. With tender compassion, the Reverend Mother explained: they had clearly felt that Heavenly Father's will was for Maria to become the wife of the Captain and the mother of his children.

There were more questions than answers in Maria's heart at that moment. She tried to understand this life-altering course. For the last several years of her young life she had felt that she was destined to serve the Lord as a celibate—it was the world she felt she had grown to understand and it was what she wanted. Now to become a baroness, a wife, a mother—was this what the Lord expected of her? The wise Abbess answered all of Maria's unasked questions by teaching her one vital principle: Heavenly Father asks us to serve Him where we are most needed and our duty and our own future happiness lies in obeying God's will cheerfully and with all of our heart.

It took a while for Maria to adapt to this new way of looking at her life. For so long she had viewed herself as a nun, a bride, not of a mortal man, but of Christ. But Georg was so patient, kind and good to his young wife. Later Maria wrote that as time passed she grew to understand and appreciate her husband's love. She grew to love him with a greater love than she had ever felt before or since. All true love, including romantic love, is a God-given gift. It is like a seed that we plant. No matter how great we think it is at first, it is but the germ of its potential. Responding to watering and nurturing, the love seeds sprout, foliate, grow and mature wonderfully. But with all of our care we do not *cause* its growth however much we facilitate it, for it is God that gives the increase and sustains its very life as He sustains every growing thing.

How did the oh-so-young Maria fare as an instant mother of seven? Certainly there were tremendous difficulties to overcome. She had succeeded as a teacher where twenty-six others had failed. But to serve as *their mother*, now that was quite another thing. Years later Maria explained that they moved onto a beautiful new level of love. Youth, by their own inexperience, are screened from fear. She felt if she would have known then all the trials and troubles of so much responsibility, perhaps she would not have dared take that step. However, adversity does not appear ominous when one is twenty.

Maria would later be criticized by some as being a strong willed and domineering mother. In the best of circumstances such accusations can be heard, sometimes even from a child whose notions cannot recognize fairly the maternal challenges and sacrifices. But these were not the best of circumstances. While Maria was putting her heart and soul into building a cohesive family the social fabric of their lives was literally torn asunder. First the von Trapps would lose their fabulous wealth. Secondly, they would be forced to either abandon their beloved Austria, or betray their honor. A strong *will* was exactly what Georg and his children needed and that is precisely what God sent them in the spunky Maria!

For a time life promised the new Baroness the fabled happily-ever-after scenario. Not only was Maria blessed with a kind and devoted husband, whose children had truly come to accept her as "Mother," but in the winter of 1929 she gave birth to a beautiful little baby girl, Rosmarie Erentrudis. This was a time of great peace for the von Trapps, a time of wonderful festivals and feasts, of traditional Austrian Christmases, where the Christ Child himself is believed to come down from Heaven on the sacred eve bringing blessings for each girl and boy. The von Trapp Christmas tree was over fifteen feet tall and was lighted by a multitude of candles on every bough. It was a time of giving, serving, sharing. Their most treasured gifts they crafted by hand for each other. It was a time of harmony as they blended their lives as well as their voices. It was an era of family activities, of campouts, of long hikes in the incomparable Austrian Alps, of quiet evenings on the shore of Zeller See, that beautiful glacier-fed lake of emerald waters. In daylight its mirrored surface reflects the grandeur of snow-capped peaks, and at night, the constellations of heaven. May of 1931 brought another beautiful daughter into their family, Eleonore (Lorli). She arrived amid the flowers of spring and the singing of the children—always the singing.

Seasons end. Placid waters are thrashed into foamy froth by the coming storm that refracts nothing but the darkness of the furious gale-swept clouds. This tempest was third in descent and in terms of destruction would far exceed its sire and grand-sire. From 900 A.D. to

1806 A.D. the remnants of the Roman Empire were gathered in the *realm* of Germanic States, ruled by a long succession of German Kings. The Second Realm was of the same lineage and engaged the entire world in a war of apocalyptic proportions. Though defeated, yet in a scarce twenty years, it bred a monstrous Third Realm—The Third Reich. Like an approaching hurricane it came. The news from their neighboring nation of the little moustached man, with his strutting army of soldiers in black uniforms bearing the symbolic death skull, were as lowering clouds and distant thunderings. Life continued as before, until suddenly Austria felt the first gusty winds. Overnight Germany forbade Austrian trade. The little country of scenic wonder is particularly dependent on tourism. Without the deutsche mark flowing across its border the Austrian banks were placed in serious jeopardy. A fierce patriot, Baron von Trapp pulled all of his tremendous wealth from the safety of a large London bank and deposited his monies in Austria, in a valiant effort to sure up the economy. But Hitler was successful in bringing "Austria to her knees"—the banks failed, Georg's money was lost! The blow was numbing to the gentle father who feared greatly for his family's welfare.

Georg reproached himself for losing most of his fortune. They must now simplify their standard of living, sell the car, close up part of the house, live basically on the third floor, and let most of the staff go. Though Georg felt deeply depressed, Maria could not despair. From the first moment of hearing about their financial loss Maria felt almost euphoric— something good would come from this apparent tragedy. This was a new beginning for her family. She had come from a harsh childhood, striking out on her own with nothing but determination to wrestle out a future. Maria tried now to encourage her husband with the same optimism, reassuring Georg that without these drastic financial reverses, they never would have learned how supportive and independent their children were. When Georg wondered at her cheerfulness, Maria replied:

> "We were not really rich, we just happened to have a lot of money. That's why we can never be poor. I am so happy to know that we don't belong to those for whom it is so hard to enter the Kingdom of God.'"

Maria's treasure was truly where her heart was. Her treasure was her faith and her family, and they were not lost. More than ever before she now was needed. For the first time in their lives, the von Trapp family would need to earn a living. Maria converted the large northwest room into a chapel and boarded a priest and several students of the Catholic University. The Villa became an inn. Within a year their villa was filled with fascinating students, scientists, writers, and professors. The family had never had such delightful discussions and fun evenings of laughter and music. The children flourished in the stimulating atmosphere and Georg and Maria knew that this treasure was worth more than gold. Through it all they continued to sing together and delight their guests.

In a day where so many value materialism above relationships, in a day when many women esteem husbands solely on capacity to provide the luxuries they demand, and in so doing teach their children ingratitude coupled with spoiled expectations—in such a day as ours, what an example is Maria! If any thought she married the older Georg for his fortune, they would have been forced to admit that she was more delighted in his misfortunes—for then she excelled as his *help*mate. How her optimism and faith blessed her children, teaching them to cast off foolish self-sufficiency and replace it with *self-reliance*. The former is haughty and denies dependence upon God while the latter honors Him as the giver of all that is good, recognizing the good even in severe trials, and unites this knowledge with individual agency and personal responsibility. Maria told her family that if they sought first to please God, and do all things for His love, that He would reward them an hundredfold, even in this life. Her paradigm became theirs. Georg and Maria began seeing this reward unfold as each child rallied, accepting new tasks and responsibilities. They, individually and collectively, reflected Maria's support of their father and were willing to work cheerfully "with rolled up shirtsleeves" in the cause of the family.

Another reward came in the form of Father Wasner, a young priest who came to officiate in their private chapel. He was very impressed with the music of the von Trapps. As an accomplished musician, he began working with them, seriously refining and sharpening their skills. In 1936, as they sang, "Jesu Meine Freude" under the pines of their estate, they were over heard by a professional singer, Lotte Lehmann. She was so enthusiastic of their talent that she herself entered them in the Salzberg group singing festival. Despite abject terror where they wished only to "evaporate," the von Trapps performed three numbers. To their complete shock, when the winners were announced, the von Trapp Family Singers were awarded first prize. This led to radio performances, a concert at the

Salzberg Festival and later to a European concert tour. They sang for kings and queens and even for Pope Pius XI. Yes, Maria had felt that something was coming. Indeed their family had stepped into a new life where they learned that music is the universal language.

On March 11, 1938 they were all gathered in their library celebrating Agathe's birthday, when over their radio they heard the programming interrupted. The Chancellor of Austria declared that their homeland had been invaded—that he was "yielding to force." They were all stunned. The radio fell silent—then moments later the silence was broken by a harsh voice barking across the air waves: "Austria is dead: Long live the Third Reich!" Suddenly, outside they could hear the church bells of Salzburg ringing and ringing and ringing. The automaton voice on the radio explained how Austria was demonstrating to the world gratitude and joy by sounding every church bell in greeting to Nazi "liberators." It was of course, a lie. The Gestapo had entered into every church and cathedral— the bell ringing was forced at the point of a gun.

The next day the city was drenched in red Swastika flags, from public buildings and private residences alike. But there was one very prominent home in Aigen that was noticeably flag free. Later, Baron von Trapp received a personal visit from a tall man attired in the foreboding dress of the Gestapo. When he asked Georg if it was true that he did not own a Nazi flag, Georg answered, "That's correct." The officer demanded to know why. Captain von Trapp did not shrink but, with characteristic courage, met the dangerous undercurrents head on. With a "dangerous twinkle in his eye" Georg told the zealous Nazi that it cost too much. The Gestapo officer left, but returned shortly with a new huge red flag bearing the ugly black German Swastika. He handed it to Georg, telling him to put it up immediately. However, the Austrian patriot politely refused. When asked why he simply replied:

> "You know, I don't like the color. It's too loud. But if you want me to decorate my house, I have beautiful oriental rugs. I can hang one from every window."

This attitude was a very dangerous one for the Baron, Maria and their family. But nothing happened. They would find out why soon enough— the Third Reich did not wish to offend the submarine commander for whom they had great plans.

Overnight everything changed. Streets were renamed after high-ranking Nazis. The children went to school only to find new teachers, teaching a new curriculum, singing a new national anthem, and worst of all, a new greeting. Austria is a deeply religious country. Their traditional salutation is *Grüss Gott*, which means *Greetings to God*. In this manner every joyful hello recognizes God, the Creator of all that we greet. Now under mandate of law, and under penalty of incarceration, the sole salutation was to be: *Heil Hitler*. Hail the man. Thus in the most personal way possible, Hitler usurped God! Soon it was forbidden to mention the word *God* or *Christ* in school or in public places—not even in Christmas songs. How offensive to the devout von Trapps!

On a daily basis Maria became more concerned for her children's welfare. In school they were being taught that Jesus Christ was "only a naughty Jewish boy who ran away from His parents." Then Maria was called into the school office. Her daughter would not repeat the new anthem and had told the entire class that her father said that he would preferably be killed and his body discarded on a "dung heap" rather than sing such noise. Maria was once again called in when, as the students were practicing the new salute, *Heil Hitler*, her little daughter compressed her lips tightly and refused to raise her hand. Maria was threatened of being reported to the authorities. This, she was told, was their last warning.

However Hitler was far more interested in Baron von Trapp than to give notice to the infractions of a school child. The Baron was a favorite son of Austria who still wielded considerable influence. What's more he had talents that could be extremely valuable to the Reich. By this time the von Trapps had become well known as a world-class family choir. The *von Trapp Family Singers* as representatives from Austria were invited to entertain the Führer at his birthday celebration. To do so would be to open the doors of fortune and fame in that part of Europe that was under Nazi control. A family council was held. The children inquired whether or not they would have to say *Heil Hitler* or sing the new national anthem. The unanimous decision was not to perform and they politely declined the invitation.

Just a few days before the invasion, Rupert graduated from Medical School. Now the Nazis offered him a leading position on the staff of a large hospital in Vienna. It was known that they were short of doctors— they had imprisoned and killed so many Jewish physicians—and it was known that the Nazis were involved in *experimental medicine*. Again, a profitable offer was refused by a member of the von Trapp family.

Later Baron von Trapp and Maria dinned at an elegant restaurant. To their surprise, Hitler was seated at the very next table. He was surrounded by SS men, all roaring with riotous laughter. The Fürher fell backward in merriment, his moustachelet quivered, his arms waving uncontrollably, he was vulgar—embarrassing. Maria remarked that it was incredulous to think that this very ordinary, foolish thug held the fate of millions in his hands.

They left the restaurant and walked in a long beautiful garden. After a moment Georg suddenly remembered a letter in his pocket. It was a "polite" offer from the Nazi Navy requesting that Captain von Trapp command a large new submarine. The letter promised advancement as he would further be called upon to establish future Adriatic and Mediterranean submarine bases. Georg's first thought was of the professional opportunity this afforded—not a captain of a forty-foot pioneer vessel, but of a sleek new state-of-the-art submarine! In the Great War his crew consisted of only five men. Now he was offered the command of a new generation U-boat, 221 feet in length manned by a crew of up to 63 sailors. The offer intimated that he would ultimately be given the authority to direct thousands as the admiral of a Mediterranean fleet! His mind racing as they walked beneath scarlet blossoming Chestnut trees, Georg told Maria of the marvelous capabilities of the new subs and of this rare opportunity he'd been given. Then he abruptly stopped. How could he think that he could ever work for the Nazis—fight for their evil cause? Georg told Maria that it was out of the question!

They changed directions in the garden walkways. Georg, still holding the letter, gazed past the vivid blossoms of the neatly trimmed flowerbeds. Trying to view this monumental decision he reasoned, No; this may be God's will. He had been continually warned that opposition to the Nazi's would bring harm to his family. If he accepted this offer, would it be the means of saving them? The Navy was his life's work, could he turn his back on the greatest professional opportunity of his life? As evil as Hitler was, was he not the Head of State, not of Germany only, but of his beloved Austria as well?

In all this Maria was silent, knowing that this "dangerously precious moment" was between Georg and the Lord—*as is any wrestle with conscience*. We brush up against Heaven's veil, searching for an answer. In the fullest sense this struggle of self will against Divine will is a battle. Jacob wrestled in the wilderness and became Israel. The location of conflicts, *where they occur,* directly influences the outcome. Thus battlefields are strategically selected. How fitting for Georg and Maria, in that weighty pivotal moment—when their individual and collective lives hung in the balance—how appropriate was their beautiful surroundings. There have been other Gardens of Decisions where eternal victories were won over evil. Why did the fall of man, the atonement and the resurrection all transpire within the setting of a garden? Mark Twain said, "Flowers catch the smile of God and preserve it." Each work of nature evidences its Creator. Thus, the natural setting becomes a temple that points the soul to God. Here too, Maria's heart echoed the sacred words uttered in another Garden as she silently prayed, "Thy will be done."

As they neared the exit Georg was deep in reverie, that spiritual stillness that allows one to feel divine direction. He turned to Maria, somewhat sadly, and told her that he could not accept the naval commission. He explained that he had taken an oath on the old Austrian flag swearing allegiance to God and his country. This, he said, would be in opposition to God and his native land. No, he told her, he couldn't do it. He would not break his former oath!

Maria knew well what this meant. She knew that they were about to lose all comforts and all possessions. To sacrifice your all for your principles is truly heroic. But it meant a great deal more than personal sacrifice for Maria—she was expecting another child. Oh, for the luxury of dealing with one trial at a time, but that was not feasible. To flee Austria, abandon home, forsake security with a baby in the womb! And this was not a typical pregnancy. In these ten years of marriage Maria had borne two girls and had suffered two miscarriages. Now this pregnancy threatened her very life. Both of Maria's kidneys were terribly, chronically infected. Recently the Doctor had told Georg and Maria: "The child has to be removed, of course, immediately." Maria was appalled at his assumption that she would so quickly submit to an abortion. There was no "of course" about it. Understanding her intent, the doctor frightened Georg with his ominous prognosis that the unborn child would *not* be born alive. The doctor ordered Maria to bed and further stated that he only hoped that he would be able to save Maria's life.

Maria, however, viewed this dangerous situation far differently. She knew the life within her was truly *life*—more precious to her than her own. Her protective motherly love for this child was there the moment she knew that *he* was there, long before his birth. Now it would be impossible for her to await his delivery resting in bed. In such dire circumstances she knew she must commence a dangerous pilgrimage. Surely the words of Christ must have sounded loudly in her mind:

"And woe unto them that are with child, and to them that give suck in those days!"

What made such courage possible? Love. True motherly love. Maria took great comfort in these words of Saint Augustine:

"Love is an excellent thing and a very great blessing, indeed. It makes every difficulty easy. It bears a burden without being weighted, and renders sweet all that is bitter. Love knows no limits, feels no burden, thinks nothing of troubles, attempts more than it is able . . . Love is like a living flame, a burning torch, it tends upward and passes unharmed through every obstacle."

To these sentiments Maria added:

"Whatever faults may be committed, big or small, whatever clouds may pile up on the horizon, dark and threatening, love will overcome all."

Georg once again called his wife and children to counsel together and explained their plight. He told the children that the Nazis had made three notable offers to the von Trapp family and when they said no this time it would be their third refusal. This was a crisis and he spoke in a voice so serious that even Maria noted his solemnity. In plain words he explained that they had an irreversible decision to make. Did they want to keep their stately home with all of its old and valuable furnishings, all of the material wealth they still had, including their lands; and did they want to remain with their friends for whom they held such deep affection? If so, then it would be necessary for them to abandon their spiritual possessions, their faith and their honor. In the situation in which they were placed, he told them, they could not longer have it both ways. With the pay he would receive from the Navy coupled with that which they were earning as classical performers they could stay in Austria and once again enjoy wealth, but he questioned whether money earned at the expense of dishonor could ever bring happiness. As their father, he taught them, he would rather lead them through poverty, if privation was required of them, in order to preserve their family's integrity. He concluded by stating that if they chose the right they would have to go. Then he asked what they wanted to do? In one voice they answered that they would follow their father! With a sense of urgency in his voice he responded:

"Then, let's get out of here soon. You can't say no three times to Hitler."

Only a few close friends and relatives were told about their plans to leave Austria. It was a time when few could be trusted—for even their butler was a Nazi. To keep the proper perspective it is important to understand that the year was 1938. Although Austria had been invaded no bullets had been fired. The country of 80 million had in one evening simply rolled its forces unexpectedly into its little neighbor of only 6 million (Hitler had *promised* Austria that he wouldn't invade). With the German occupation impediments had been lifted and the economy was rebounding and Hitler had promised a peace for the Germanic people that would last a thousand years! Universally, the von Trapps were told by these confidants that it would be totally irresponsible to uproot their children and lead them into an uncertain future—to do so, they said, would be completely "wrong."

There will always be conflicting voices, whose admonishments will oppose the right course of action. However, that Voice which speaks to the heart and whose warmth is felt in the deepest recesses of the soul was the only Voice that Georg, Maria and their family would listen to. Later these same friends would sadly admit, after having lost that which can never be replaced, that the von Trapps had chosen the far better path. But now there was no time to lose. In all outward appearances they were preparing to embark upon a short hiking holiday to the Alps. Only individual rucksacks were taken—all else was left behind. They boarded the train at the village station and left. Hours later they crossed the Italian border— and that was it. Having sacrificed all worldly possessions as literally as if they had been forced from their mansion at gunpoint, having left all things comfortable and familiar, having fled their homeland entirely on their own volition—to uphold faith and honor—the von Trapp family had become refugees, possessing only what they wore on their backs and in their hearts.

The first station on their journey, after leaving Nazi-infested Austria, was a beautiful mountain village in the province of Tyrol in Southern Italy. There were twelve souls in this company of self-exiles—Georg, Maria, nine children (soon to be ten), and Father Wasner. They had no sooner arrived at a peaceful inn on the outskirts of this little town when suddenly six year old Lorli began to sob and wail. Somehow in their flight her favorite toy, a lumpy old teddy bear, had been left behind. Although still very young herself, Maria had come to truly understand the tender feelings of children. Later, when writing of this experience, she explained that a child is capable of feeling grief with all of her heart. Therefore we should never dismiss the bottomless hurt they feel as insignificant. Children, she said, live mainly in the present. They do not remember or understand their past experiences as well as we do and they are also far less capable of comprehending future hope. Therefore, if the *present* is awful, disastrous, a child is truly helpless and totally dependent on mother and father. Maria said that unless we immediately come to her aid, the child will suffer with her "whole little being."

In her own words she says:

"I remember the situation so well, the glassed-in veranda in which we were standing, and me looking for a cookie or a candy, and there was none. Had I forgotten that we were refugees now, and luxuries like candies were things of the past? But even if the hands of a mother are empty, her mind and heart must never be. Taking the sobbing little girl on my lap, I said, 'Come, Lorli, Mother is going to tell you a story.'"

This chapter honors the exemplary young heroine who chose the highest calling a woman can accept in her life's mission. Maria chose Motherhood. Although her hands were emptied, again and again—her mind and heart never were! On that fateful day, on the mountain slopes of Italy, with Lorli on her lap and her head against her bosom, Maria told her children of another refugee family—a family like theirs that had fled the Hitler and Gestapo of their day. She told them of a dangerous flight into Egypt, of braving horrific heat at midday and bitter cold at midnight, of the menace of wild animals and murderous bandits —all for the sake of principle—and all to fulfill a Life's mission. She told them that Herod is really never dead in this world, and that he still "seeks the Child to destroy Him." She gave her little ones the comfort of being "fellow refugees" to the Most High God.

All else that Maria did in life, with her music, her New Guinea missionary efforts later in life, and even the humanitarian aid that the von Trapps brought to their fellow countrymen after the war through their *Austrian Relief Fund*, a fund that provided for some 20,000 families—all else that she ever accomplished is subordinate to Maria's noble Motherhood. Little Gusti, child of the Mountains, became the Matriarch Maria, the mother of a great posterity. She instilled in the lives of her children, and her children's children, that they too should look to the Mountain, the Faithful Guardian of their lives, the Rock of Salvation.

The von Trapps had left their house, but never would they leave their home. As John Ruskin explains:

"This is the true nature of home—it is the place of peace; the shelter, not only from all injury, but from all terror, doubt, and division. In so far as it is not this, it is not home: so far as the anxieties of the outer life penetrate into it, and the inconsistently-minded, unknown, unloved, or hostile society of the outer world is allowed by either husband or wife to cross the threshold, it ceases to be home; it is then only a part of that outer world which you have roofed over, and lighted fire in. But so far as it is a sacred place, a vestal temple, a temple of the hearth watched over by Household Gods, before whose faces none may come but those whom they can receive with love,—so far as it is this, and roof and fire are types only of a nobler shade and light,—shade as of the rock in a weary land, and light as of the Pharos in the stormy sea,—so far it vindicates the name, and fulfills the praise, of home.

"And wherever a true wife [and mother] comes, this home is always round *her*. The stars only may be over her head; the glowworm in the night-cold grass may be the only fire at her foot: but home is yet wherever she is. . ."

Literally with the stars as their covering and the grass their carpet, Maria made a home for her wandering family.

It would have been impossible for the von Trapps to remain in their luxurious villa and preserve their home. They had not the power to keep terror, doubt and evil outside of their palatial walls. What became of the Villa von Trapp? This beautiful mansion became the *house* and headquarters of Hitler's Second-In-Command, the most notorious mass murderer of all time, Heinrich Himmler. After World War II, the Americans returned the Villa to the von Trapps—but they would never live there again. After *incomprehensible evil* had desecrated their former home this noble family knew of only one way to cleanse its confines. They sold the estate to their church to be utilized as a seminary.

Today it is known as the Kolleg St. Josef. Father Audreas Hasenburger now presides over this academy. He is a kindly and devout priest, who not only loves his order, but the beautiful college of faith in which he lives and works. Darkness cannot remain where there is light—and peace has returned to the Villa von Trapp. Himmler's office is now a sacred chapel and his casino is now a lovely dining room. Although one can easily *picture* in the mind's eye the terrible crimes committed on these grounds by the Nazis, that is not what you *feel* when you enter this imposing manor. You feel you have entered a place sanctified by the godly service of good men and good women. Thanks to this peace, the walls again resonate sounds only the heart can hear—harmonies of the best of times long gone-by—sweet strains from the strings of Georg's violin, the golden voices of the children, the melodious tones of Maria's guitar. Consider also that within these walls Maria truly commenced her life's mission. Aunt Lizzy, of the Doktorwirt, remembers the youthful mother—how on beautiful Sunday mornings she would see Maria, with her covey of children trailing behind, walking across the meadow from the Villa to the Schloss Chapel. Lizzy was a very young girl then and thought it exceptional that the Baroness was so kind and cheerful. She reminisced how they would line up in the chapel choir, so many for one family, and fill the air with glorious music.

When the von Trapps lost their fortune and abandoned their estate to their enemies, the future looked precarious, to say the least. Singing would ultimately prove to be their temporal salvation. At the Salzburg Festivals concert managers from around the globe were in attendance and were extremely impressed with the von Trapp's talent. They received so many foreign invitations, all of which at the time they never intended to accept, that they pasted them in a scrapbook. Most of what they put into their rucksacks when they left Austria was of little value—but in Georg's pack was the scrapbook—providing contacts for concerts—one was from America. After extraordinary effort and sacrifice the von Trapps arrived in the United States with only four dollars in their pockets. Maria worked closely with this American agent, and tirelessly motivated her family to establish themselves in the entertainment business. When their resources were sufficient, they purchased land in the mountains of Stowe, Vermont, and with their own hands built an Austrian Chalet. They cultivated their land into a working farm, nurturing and personally harvesting the crops as a family; the Chalet evolved into a music camp and then a ski lodge, restaurant and gift store. The von Trapps lived lives of wonderful contrast—singing before heads of state and returning to their Vermont farm to pitch hay or serve hotel guests.

On May 30, 1947 Georg, the noble hero of Maria, of his family, and of Austria, passed from this life. Though this valiant soldier did not die *in* battle, he died *from* battle. The toxic fumes that often swept through his U-Boat during World War I caused his eventual cancer and death. He was laid to rest on the flowering mountainside above their farm. Upon his chest was placed the Maria Theresien Cross and upon his knees—his beloved Austrian flag.

When the family choir finally dissolved after twenty years, Maria became a missionary in New Guinea, along with Father Wasner and three of her children, Maria, Rose Mary and Johannes. Through the light of Christianity they assisted in the transformation of the New Guinea people. For one year Maria traveled among these Melanesian people and had incredible adventures. However, her children stayed longer—Johannes served for three and a half years, Rose Mary for five and Maria the younger remained in the islands for *ten* years! Truly this mother implanted the virtue of self-sacrifice in the hearts of her children. Maria has authored at least four wonderful books that detail her life and ideals. These are hard to find treasures, unless you visit the von Trapp Family Gift Store in Stowe.

In 1987, forty years after Georg's death; Maria—Gusti—died. She was laid beside her beloved Georg. Together they rest in the bosom of the mountains.

"When you are a child of the mountains yourself, you really belong to them. You need them. They become the faithful guardians of your life. . . ."

Bibliography
Primary Sources
Von Trapp, Maria: *Maria, My Own Story*
Von Trapp, Maria: *Yesterday, Today & Forever* (New Leaf Press, Green Forest AR)
Trapp, Maria Augusta: *The Story Of The Trapp Family Singers* (Doubleday, New York)
Ruskin, John: *Harvard Classics, Volume 28* (P. F. Collier & Son Corporation, New York)
First hand research was accomplished in Salzburg, Aigen and Zell am See by the Author, with the able assistance of his sister, Susan Hancock.

Lady Jane

When I come to the end of my journey I shall obtain that which has been the pursuit of my life.

Beneath the altar pavement of the small chapel of St Peter ad Vincula in England lies the body of a petite sixteen year old girl. On either side of her rests the bodies of Queen Katherine and Queen Anne who perished on the scaffold of the Tower of London. Lord Macaulay said of this melancholy place, "In truth there is no sadder spot on the earth than [this] little cemetery." Why would he feel such grief within these medieval walls? Why are the stone arches of this ancient chapel bent in reverent sorrow? Who is this young maiden who ranks royal interment? Her name is Lady Jane Grey and she too is a Queen, and far more a queen than her regal companions. For Jane was Sovereign of her soul. And she too died upon the bloody scaffold of the infamous Tower. But unlike Katherine and Anne, Jane died a heroine, a martyr, and chose death rather than renounce her faith and religion.

Jane was born in October of 1537 in the reign of King Henry the VIII. Her grandmother was Mary Tudor, sister of the King. Her father was Henry Grey, Duke of Suffolk. Amidst such royalty and in the splendor of Bradgate, her ancestral home, Jane was raised, but her life was anything but pampered. Her parents could envision but one future for her—Queen of England! Although her position at birth placed her in the royal line of succession, after her cousins, Edward, Mary, Elizabeth and her mother Frances—her parents sought a far more immediate ascension to the throne. Edward was the same age as Jane and what her mother and father desired most was their marriage. This was not an unselfish motive; there was no thought of what would be best for their little girl. Her mother, Frances Grey, was a woman of avarice and was greedy for power, riches and prestige. She ruled her house as a tyrant and was particularly cruel to Jane. Henry Grey, her father, was self-indulgent and sought to ever increase his ease and affluence through his wife's blood line. It was unlikely that Frances Grey would outlive the younger heirs to the crown and she did not want to wait an inordinate amount of time anyway. Nor did she want the incredibly restrictive responsibility that falls upon a monarch. She saw the perfect solution to her ambition in her daughter and was ever aided in her scheme by her husband.

From the cradle, then, Jane was raised to be Queen, wife of King Edward the VI. From her earliest recollections her mother required absolute perfection of her and if she failed in the least degree severe punishments followed. Each morning Jane would rise at six and after breakfast she was required to visit her parents for what they ironically called her "daily blessing" (for these blessings were often beatings). Her activities of the yesterday were reviewed followed by crushing criticisms and frequent blows to her little frame. Her life was anything but what one might imagine the life of a princess to be.

At age four Jane's formal education began. One might think that to begin serious studies so early in life might be further abuse, but in this case it would prove to be Jane's salvation and the fountain of her happiness. To make her the fit mate for a king, Henry Grey hired his chaplain, a youthful Cambridge scholar named John Aylmer to be Jane's tutor. John Aylmer was full of life and laughter and was devoutly religious. He was small in stature but large in spirit. He loved his little charge and as he would teach Jane he would carry her about in his arms.

John Aylmer's kindness and his skill as a teacher kindled in her a love of learning that, coupled with her innate intellect, made of her a child prodigy. The Lady Elizabeth, who years later became Queen Elizabeth the First, was also extremely intelligent—as was Edward, her brother. But Jane excelled them both. John Aylmer praised her, encouraged her and was careful in his critiques of her progress to motivate and never discourage her. The time they spent together was a total reprieve from an otherwise intolerable existence. In the morning she was taught Latin, Greek and Hebrew. In the afternoon she would study modern languages, which besides English would include lessons in French, Spanish, German, etc. She was taught to read each day from the Holy Scriptures and to love the truths found in sacred writ. She was also schooled in the Classics and was soon reading them in the original language and making translations into her own tongue. After the evening meal she would practice dancing and do needlework, retiring to her bed at 9:00 p.m. So much did she enjoy her studies that she preferred them above all other diversions.

As Jane grew older, she grew in wisdom and came to appreciate the contrasts in her life—the contradistinction of her cruel parents and the Christ-like manner of her tutor. These contrasts, she felt, were a blessing. John Aylmer had spoken a great deal to Jane about his friend and fellow scholar, Roger Ascham, who was tutor to Lady Elizabeth. So highly recommended was Ascham to Jane and so genuine his manner, that when he called at Bradgate to visit the Greys, she confided to him her innermost joys and pains. Jane was at this time twelve years of age. Ascham wrote tenderly of their meeting:

"Before I went into Germany, I came to Bradgate . . . to take my leave of that noble Lady Jane Grey, to whom I am exceeding much beholding. Her parents, the Duke and Duchess with all the household, Gentlemen and Gentlewomen, were hunting in the Park. I found her, in her Chamber, reading [Plato's] *Phaedo* in Greek, and that with as much delight, as some gentleman would read a merry tale in Boccaccio.

After salutation, and duty done, with some other talk, I asked her, 'Why madam, do you relinquish such pastimes as going into the park?' Smiling, she answered me: 'All their sport in the Park is but a shadow to that pleasure that I find in Plato. Alas! Good folk, they never felt what true pleasure meant.'

'And how came you, madam,' quoth I, 'to this deep knowledge of pleasure, and what did chiefly allure you unto it; seeing not many women, but very few men, have attained thereunto?'

'I will tell you,' quoth she, 'and tell you a truth which perchance ye will marvel at. One of the greatest benefits that ever God gave me is that he sent me so sharp and severe Parents, and so gentle a Schoolmaster. For when I am in presence either of father or mother, whether I speak, keep silence, sit, stand, or go, eat, drink, be merry, or sad, be sewing, playing, dancing, or doing anything else: I must do it, as it were, in such weight, measure, and number, even as perfectly as God made the world; or else I am so sharply taunted, so cruelly threatened, yea presently some times with pinches, nips and bobs, and other ways I will not name for the honor I bear them, so without measure misordered, that I think myself in hell, till time come that I must go to Mister Aylmer, who teacheth me so gentle, so pleasantly, with such faire allurements to learning, that I think all the time nothing, whiles I am with him. And when I am called from him, I fall on weeping, because whatsoever I do else, but learning, is full of grief, trouble, fear, and whole misliking.'

I remember that talk gladly, because it is so worthy of memory, and because also, it was the last talk that ever I had, and the last time that ever I saw that noble and worthy lady."

Jane was a lovely girl, small boned, "prettily shaped" and graceful. She had sandy hair and freckles, a "well made nose" and full red lips. Her eyes were especially beautiful with high arched eyebrows, in color darker than her hair. She was humble, quick to see the good and beautiful, and was slow to speak ill of anyone. She was precocious, witty, and particularly in matters she viewed as false she could be decisive and sharp tongued. This last attribute was clearly demonstrated as she visited the Chapel at *Beaulieu* with Princess Mary's friend, the Lady Wharton. In the royal household there were strong opposing beliefs regarding true religion. Mary, whose mother was the Spanish Kathrine of Aragon, was a staunch Catholic. Edward, Elizabeth and Jane were devout Protestants— and of the three Jane was the most pious. She regarded effigies of Christ and Mary as graven images, prohibited by scripture. She abhorred the Catholic doctrine of transubstantiation, the belief that the bread and wine of the Lord's Supper are transformed into the actual body and blood of Jesus, although their appearances remains the same. As Lady Jane and Lady Wharton walked through Beaulieu Chapel, Lady Wharton curtseyed at the altar.

"Is the Princess in the chapel?" Jane asked

"No," Lady Wharton replied.

"Then why do you curtsey?"

"I curtsey," said Lady Wharton, "to Him that made me."

"Nay," Jane said, "But did not the baker make him?"

Jane knew that Princess Mary was not in the chapel and that Lady Wharton curtseyed to the lifeless image of Christ. Her question to Lady Wharton was her direct way of pointing out her belief that it was sacrilege to bend to an effigy. Her implication was certainly understood by Lady Wharton whose answer made her more vulnerable still to Jane's quick wit. In one swift sentence Jane refers to the Eucharist and the concept of transubstantiation. Saying in effect, "You say the Lord made you, but when you take the sacramental bread you believe it to be the actual flesh of Christ—did not the baker make the bread? Is it not ridiculous to think that a baker makes the body of the Lord? Surely the bread is an emblem only of the flesh of Christ." That this conversation has been preserved in history is evidence that Lady Wharton certainly brought this offense to Mary's attention furthering the rift between Catholic Mary and Protestant Jane.

Although raised by the Duke and Duchess as a princess, dressed in rich silks, damasks and velvets, as she grew older Jane gravitated towards the simple attire that she felt was more becoming a Protestant maiden. Once when Jane was to attend a reception held in honor of the Queen Regent of Scotland, Princess Mary made her an elegant gift, a fantastic gown of tinsel cloth of gold and velvet overlaid with a parchment lace of gold. Jane was anything but delighted. Her nurse, Mrs. Ellen was overjoyed as she presented the gown to Jane.

"What shall I do with it?" Jane asked.

"Wear it, to be sure," her nurse wonderingly replied.

Appalled, Jane declared, "Nay, that were a shame to follow my Lady Mary against God's word."

Far more than an avowal of godly fashion this statement foreshadowed the ultimate cause of her death yet a few short years in the future.

Her developing intellect and spiritual convictions are clearly seen in a letter Jane wrote to Chief Pastor Bullinger of Zurich.

"You exhort me to embrace a genuine and sincere faith in Christ my savior. I will endeavor to satisfy you in this respect, as far as God shall enable me to do. But as I acknowledge faith to be his gift, I ought therefore only to promise so far as He may see fit to bestow it upon me. I shall not, however, cease to pray with the apostles, that He may of his goodness daily increase it in me... Do, meanwhile, with your wonted kindness make daily mention of me in your prayers. In the study of Hebrew I shall pursue that method which you so clearly point out."

Later she wrote to this distinguished man of letters:

"Were I to extol you, as truth requires, I should need either the oratorical powers of Demosthenes, or the eloquence of Cicero. In writing to you in this manner I have exhibited more boldness than prudence...but so great has been your kindness to me, in condescending to write to me, a stranger, and in supplying the necessary instructions for the adornment of my understanding and the improvement of my mind...Besides, I entertain the hope that you will excuse the more than feminine boldness of me, who, girlish and unlearned as I am, presume to write to a man who is the father of learning...

My mind is fluctuating and undecided; for while I consider my age, sex and mediocrity, or rather, infancy of learning, each of these things deters me from writing, but when I call to mind the eminence of your virtues, the celebrity of your character, and the magnitude of your favors towards me...the respect which your merits demand usually prevails over all other considerations...

As long as I shall be permitted to live, I shall not cease to offer you my good wishes, to thank you for the kindness you have showed me, and to pray for your welfare.

Farewell learned sir.

Your piety's most devoted,

Jane Grey

In reading these letters to Bullinger we must remind ourselves that they were penned by a very young Jane. She humbly proclaims herself "girlish" and "unlearned." Yet the opposite is certainly true. She demonstrates a formidable intellect and a command of language representative of a scholar. With wisdom far beyond her years she considers the "adornment of [her] understanding and the improvement of [her] mind" her greatest task. Most girls and women of her class cared far more to adorn their bodies with costly array and neglected terribly their most precious possessions—mind and soul. Not so with Jane! She prayed daily for Heavenly Father to increase her faith in her Savior. That God answered her prayers and granted her extraordinary faith was ultimately proven in the manner in which she laid down her life. And when that time came and she passed gloriously the greatest test that anyone could face in this life, she took with her to the next world one true possession—a mind adorned with faith and intelligence!

When we look for brilliance in Britannia in the age of the Tudors, we find it not in the Church, the Parliament, or in the Palace; not among the aged educated in Cambridge. But radiance we find truly in young and tender age in the brilliant Jane Grey.

Centuries earlier a young man named Elihu the Buzite discovered the secret of acquiring wisdom and understanding while in his youth—the same secret that Jane knew. Elihu said:

"I [am] young, and ye [are] very old; wherefore I was afraid, and durst not shew you mine opinion. I said, Days should speak, and multitude of years should teach wisdom. But [there is] a spirit in man: and the inspiration of the Almighty giveth them understanding. Great men are not [always] wise: neither do the aged (when uninspired) understand judgment."

The Glory of God is intelligence and he delights to bestow understanding, just as he delights to bestow faith, upon those who diligently seek it. One can never be truly great in any field without the inspiration of the Almighty. What is more, Jane was truly beautiful because she was truly virtuous. Beauty is the mark God puts on Virtue.

She believed in the Bible's injunction to honor her parents, and as we will later see, did so despite absolute betrayal by her father. There were many in her time, as there are in our time, which believed the Bible's idealistic values impossible to adhere to. The commandments, they say, were given to us mere humans to prove that we could not keep them, and thus they pervert the doctrine of Grace. But Jane believed that if God gave a commandment he would prepare a way for her to live it—even if her living the Lord's command meant her death.

When Jane and Edward were nine, King Henry VIII died. Edward then became King Edward VI of England; but of course he was too young to rule. His father had foreseen this difficulty and had formed a council to govern the throne until Edward became of age to rule. The most prominent members of the council were Edward Seymour and John Duddley. Seymour was the uncle of the boy-king, being the brother of his mother (Jane Seymour). Edward Seymour was proclaimed by his fellow councilors to be Lord Protector of England and Governor of the King's Person.

Jane's life also changed dramatically shortly thereafter. Jane was sent to live with King Henry VIII's widow, Katherine Parr, the Queen Dowager. The time she spent with Katherine was probably the happiest of her life. Queen Katherine had no authority in the government which was ruled by the Lord Protector, and her time therefore, was her own. Katherine was loving and kind and welcomed Jane with open arms. Jane was famished for female affection and motherly love which the Queen gladly imparted. Not only did she nurture Jane emotionally, but Katherine increased the depth of Jane's spiritual convictions. The Queen Dowager, like Jane's tutor, was a sincere Protestant. She praised Jane for her mental competence and skill and Katherine's ladies openly foretold that one day she would be Queen herself.

Before her marriage to King Henry VIII, Katherine Parr had been betrothed to Thomas Seymour, brother of Edward Seymour the Lord Protector. After the King's death, Katherine was soon courted again by Thomas and her old love for him quickly rekindled. They were married a few months later.

Thomas Seymour was also a member of the Council and was Lord High Admiral of the British Navy. He was fiercely ambitious and was extremely jealous of his brother the Lord Protector. It is hard to imagine the ends to which some people will go to realize their desire for power and cupidity. Thomas betrayed his country, betrayed the lives of his subordinate seamen into the hands of pirates, and sought to use Jane Grey and the boy King Edward to realize his dream of dominion. First he purchased, for a considerable sum, the wardship of Jane from her father making himself her guardian—with the promise that he would ensure that Jane would marry Edward VI. Then he began to give Edward VI enormous amounts of spending money (although King, he was still a boy and his purse strings were tightly controlled by the Lord Protector) to poison Edward's mind against the Lord Protector.

His next move was to raise, by nefarious means, funds for an army of mercenaries to fight his brother, the Lord Protector, for control of the throne. It would take an incredible amount of money for men and arms. He blackmailed the vice-treasurer of Bristol Mint, obtaining a huge sum. He formed a confederacy with pirates to plunder English Ships for a share of the booty and gave them sanctuary in his own lands in the Scilly Isles. Certainly as Lord High Admiral he was able to provide all the details necessary to minimize their risks and maximize their take. How many lives were lost because of his treachery may not be known, but there were many. He also extorted money from merchant vessels in return for safe passage. He had counterfeit keys made of the royal privy gardens, next to Edward VI's chambers, and he obtained a forgery of the King's signature stamp.

Thomas' desired end to these schemes was simply fantastic! He planned to kidnap Edward, supposedly to save him from a deadly intrigue by the Lord Protector, marry him to his ward, the Lady Jane Grey and assume the role of Lord Protector. In the inevitable battle that would follow with Edward Seymour, the ruling Lord Protector, he would defend himself, King Edward and Lady Jane with his own army. The King would be in his custody, married to his ward, which would give him considerable advantage.

This was not all—Katherine Parr died on September 5, 1548 after giving birth. Thomas, meanwhile, was amorously involved with fourteen year old Elizabeth and planned to take her as his own bride. Think of the consolidation of power! Protector of the Realm, Guardian of the King and his own ward Jane, Queen by marriage, and husband to Elizabeth, heir to the throne in her own right! To Thomas Seymour this was worth everything—his honor, the destruction of his own family, the lives of countless subjects, and the loss of his own soul.

On the night of January 16, 1549, Thomas Seymour attempted to kidnap his nephew, the young King Edward. He entered the King's quarters at Hampton Court through the privy garden but was attacked by Edward's dog. He shot the dog but the report brought the King's Guard immediately to his bedside. The plot had failed. Thomas was investigated, committed to the tower, charged with treason, plotting to overthrow his brother, marry the Lady Jane to the King and take Elizabeth for his own bride. Two months later, on March 20, he was beheaded on the scaffold of the Tower.

Poor Jane! A pawn in the hands of her parents. A short respite under the motherly and loving influence of Katherine Parr, now dead—then under the control of wicked Thomas Seymour. With his execution Jane was returned to Bradgate Manor. Her parents, The Duke and Duchess of Suffolk, were angry and bitter. They had come so close to their lofty aspirations! Jane became the brunt of their displeasure and was again severely abused by them. Her only solace was her education and her ever-faithful friend and tutor, John Alymer.

There is another tragic postscript to this era. As stated earlier, Katherine Parr had died giving birth. The child born to Katherine Parr and Thomas Seymour was a baby girl named Mary. The orphaned infant, although the daughter of a Queen and the Lord High Admiral, was left without any estate, her father's property confiscated by Attainder. Soon after her birth those who cared for her complained regarding her expense and requested an allowance from the Lord Protector. It appears that none was granted and it is also likely that Mary Seymour did not live beyond her first birthday.

Little wonder then that Jane Grey also could turn to no other person. There was no family that cared for her needs or her happiness. There was no person in authority who would protect her rights. Few poor souls are ever so unfortunate! Jane was a commodity, something useful that could be turned into commercial advantage. Had she reached the age and circumstance of majority she certainly would have taken charge of her mortal destiny and would have proven a great blessing to countless others. Had she truly reigned as Queen she would have blessed the nations! The person who can rule self can rule kingdoms and Jane perfectly governed Jane. And thus in her extremities she found that there was One who would never fail; One who would always comfort, understand, guide, direct and love. He was the only One whom she could trust and the only One who would uphold her. Sadly, in her life, this was literally true. A few short years later when Jane was imprisoned in the Tower she wrote a letter to her sister Katherine Grey in the cover of her New Testament which she presented to her sister as a farewell gift.

"I have sent you, good sister Katherine, a book, which although it be not outwardly trimmed with gold, yet inwardly it is more worth than precious stones. It is the book, dear sister, of the laws of the lord: It is His Testament and Last Will, which He bequeathed unto us wretches, which shall lead you to the path of eternal joy, and if you, with a good mind read it, and with an earnest desire, follow, it shall bring you to an immortal and everlasting life.

"It will teach you to live and learn you to die...[Your convictions in this Testament] shall win you more than you should have gained by the possession of your woeful father's lands ...[Within its covers are] such riches as neither the covetous shall withdraw from you, neither the thief shall steal, neither let the moth corrupt...And as touching my death, rejoice as I do and consider that I shall be delivered of this corruption and put on incorruption, for as I am assured that I shall for losing of a mortal life, find an immortal felicity. Pray God grant you and send you his grace...

"Farewell good sister, put only your trust in God, who only must uphold you,

Your loving sister, Jane Duddley."

You will note that the letter is signed "Jane *Duddley*." How did Jane, still so very young, become a Duddley? You will remember that when King Henry VIII formed the council to rule until Edward became of age to reign there were two prominent members: Edward Seymour who became Lord Protector and John Duddley. After Thomas Seymour's execution, his brother Edward was caught in the wake of scandal. Quickly John Duddley railed support to depose Edward Seymour and promote himself. Armed conflict followed and Edward Seymour was forced to surrender. Not long afterwards John Duddley ruled England without the consent of Parliament and without the pretense of the office of Lord Protector, but as sole Dictator. He was the most wicked man to govern Britain in the Sixteenth Century. Duddley used every artifice to flatter King Edward who was still a minor. Duddley so manipulated him that Edward thought he was beginning to govern his realm when in reality John Duddley ruled supreme.

Jane Grey continued her studies with excellence and was blossoming into maturity. Intellectually she had few peers. She was now fluent in Greek and Latin and through her correspondence with scholars was celebrated throughout European academia. Her fame was remarkable for any woman in that era, let alone a girl in her mid-teens. In the aftermath of the Lord Seymour scandal, Jane was betrothed to the fifteen year old son of the Duke of Somerset. However, Lady Jane was far more interested in her studies than in romance. Being a princess of royal blood her marriage would not be a matter of her choice. The betrothal to Somerset was canceled and superceded by John Duddley who once again saw in Jane a pawn for his own purposes.

Edward VI had been healthy and robust all of his life until April of 1552 when he fell seriously ill with smallpox. He never completely recovered and a year later was diagnosed with consumption, tuberculosis. With his death the crown would pass to the adult Mary who would neither need Duddley nor allow his presence in the government. Duddley knew that Mary, if she became Queen, would depose of all Protestant's in power and would restore the papal influence to Parliament. Duddley had persecuted Mary and for personal gain had promoted Protestantism by seizing Catholic properties. Neither could he allow Elizabeth, second in line of succession to ascend to the throne. Although she was a protestant she was also older (four years older than Jane) and could reign independent of him.

Now, it appeared, that his sovereignty would end with the death of King Edward, and most likely his very life. But John Duddley, Duke of Northumberland, was a man of evil cunning. Edward VI was devoutly protestant and was well aware of his sister Mary's firm adherence to Catholicism and her intolerance for heretics of that faith. Duddley persuaded Edward to make a new will disinheriting his sisters Mary and Elizabeth. He further convinced the dying boy-king to proclaim that his successor be the faithful and intelligent Lady Jane Grey. Edward respected and loved Jane immensely and knew that she was extremely capable to govern as Queen. What he did not realize was that since Jane was a minor, Duddley planned for her to rule only as his puppet and would end her life the moment she threatened his supremacy. How could he then continue his reign, you might ask, if Jane were murdered? He would marry Jane, before her ascendancy to the throne, to his fifteen-year old son, Guildford, who would then become King. In short order he would then manipulate Parliament into granting Guildford true governmental authority. His son was self-indulgent, petulant and would forever be his to control!

In careful haste, Duddley put his plan into effect. The King's decree was in fact illegal. Edward was still a minor and although the Council unanimously signed allegiance to this device, ultimately along with one hundred peers, archbishops, bishops, and knights (under terrible threat by their Dictator), Parliament did not. But Duddley cared little for legalities, and as he had ruled without effective opposition to that time, he felt invulnerable. This was not an immediate undertaking and it took some time to coerce this support. He approached the Duke and Duchess of Suffolk with his scheme, knowing that they would be delighted to see their aspirations of Jane becoming Queen finally realized. He was right, of course.

When Henry and Frances Grey informed Jane that her marriage to Somerset was canceled and that she was to marry Guildford Duddley she was absolutely appalled! She hated the Duddley family. She was only fifteen but, being highly intelligent and mature far beyond her years, she knew that such a match could bring her only misery or worse. She knew the evil character of John Duddley, the Dictator of her beloved country.

And although Guildford was tall and aristocratically handsome Jane knew that he was his father's son—vain, ambitious and potentially wicked. Jane had always been obedient to her parents—as she knew this was commanded in scripture. But this was not honoring them! She recognized this would bring terrible *dis*honor as it would be untrue to her personal faith and convictions of righteousness. She vehemently rebelled against her mother and father who could scarce believe that Jane would defy them. How could she, they thought, after all they had done for her! In a rage of fury and cursing they demanded that she obey them. For the first time in her life, she quietly responded that she would not. It was then she was beaten and whipped, perhaps more brutally than ever before. Finally, they were successful and poor Jane submitted. Her engagement to Guildford was announced in April and Jane was married to the dolt on Sunday, May 25, 1553.

After the wedding ceremony Jane returned to live with her parents for they and Duddley determined that the marriage should not be consummated until their coup was sure to succeed. Handily, it could be annulled if their stratagem did not develop as they desired. What Duddley needed was time—at this point he did not have the signatures on the King's proclamation of succession that he deemed necessary. Edward VI was on the verge of death and the Dictator could not allow him to die until every piece of his cunning plan was in place. How did he preserve the dying king's life for a few precious weeks? He dismissed the doctors and engaged a female quack who administered a poisonous potion containing arsenic to Edward. The concoction had the desired effect of keeping the boy alive, but the side effects were ghastly, causing him to tremble in agony. However, at length the final draft of Edward's "My Devise for the Succession" was written by his own tremulous hand appointing Lady Jane his successor and describing his sisters Mary and Elizabeth as "illegitimate and not lawfully begotten . . . disabled to claim the said imperial crown . . . [being] but of half blood." On the June 21, 1553 Duddley had the signatures of more than five score nobles affixed to this document and sworn to support "Jane the Queen to the uttermost of their power and never at any time to swerve from it." This, in spite of the Lord Chief Justice, the Solicitor General and the Attorney General's stated opinion, to the rage of Duddley, that these actions constituted treason. In the mean time Duddley ordered his son Guildford to consummate his marriage with Lady Jane.

It would now be only days until Edward VI would be dead and the boy prayed to God Almighty that He would release him from his intense suffering. He anguished:

"Lord God, deliver me out of this miserable and wretched life, and take me amongst Thy chosen; howbeit, not my will but Thy will be done. Lord, I commit my spirit to Thee. . . for Thy Son Jesus Christ's sake, Amen."

In the early evening of July 6, 1553 Edward VI's life ended in a rage of pain. His withered frame was evidently horrific and Duddley did not dare let his remains be seen but had "buried him privately in a paddock adjoining the palace, and substituted in his place, to be seen by the people, a young man not very unlike him, whom [he] had murdered." Duddley kept the death secret for two days while he tidied things up. All was going according to his plans.

Jane had become very ill as well. She was pale and nauseous and was losing hair. She believed that her father-in-law was slowly poisoning her. On July 9 Duddley sent his daughter to escort Jane to his mansion, Syon House on the Thames. She complained that she was very ill and could not make the journey. She was told that this was the King's command, and not knowing of his death, felt obligated to obey as an obedient subject to his Majesty. What happened next to Jane was like a surreal dream. Her head spun with sickness. She arrived in the great hall of Syon House and was left alone with Mary Duddley for a time but did not feel up to conversation. They sat in silence. After a period of time had gone by, the Dictator, John Duddley, entered the hall accompanied by members of the Council. Conversations ensued but did not directly involve Jane. Then a tribute by Lords Huntingdon and Pembroke both shocked Jane and proved a harbinger of that which was to shortly follow—they knelt before her in the veneration due a Queen and kissed her hand as Jane later said, "with unwonted caresses they did me such reverence as was not at all suitable to my state . . . making semblance of honoring me." She was further distressed when someone alluded to her as "their sovereign lady." She was then ushered to the Chamber of State and led inexorably by Duddley to the vacant throne. In this Chamber, standing by rank of nobility were many nobles, including her parents who as she passed all bowed or cursteyed. She was reeling, shaking, and in this dream-state heard Duddley announce:

"As President of the Council I do now declare the death of his most blessed and gracious Majesty, King Edward VI. We have cause to rejoice for the virtuous and praiseworthy life that His Majesty hath led, as also for his very good death . . . and for the very great care he hath taken of his kingdom at the close of his life, having prayed God to defend it from the popish faith and to deliver it from the rule of his evil sisters."

Duddley then addressed Jane directly.

"His Majesty hath named Your Grace as the heir to the crown of England! This declaration hath been approved by all the lords of the Council, most of the peers, and all the judges of the land. There is nothing wanting but Your Grace's grateful acceptance of the high estate which God Almighty, the sovereign and disposer of all crowns and scepters—never sufficiently to be thanked by you for so great a mercy—hath advanced you to. Therefore you should cheerfully take upon you the name, title and estate of Queen of England, receiving at our hands the first fruits of our humble duty."

Dazed and speechless fifteen year old Jane looked upon her parents, members of the Council, Lords and Ladies, who all knelt before her swearing their blood in her defense as their Monarch! It was more than she could bear and she fainted. She fell to the floor unassisted. No one moved forward to soften the fall. When she recovered her consciousness and looking up to this august assemblage, being cold, hurt, confused, ill— it was too much and lying upon the floor, she wept. Still no one assisted her, but left her comfortless. At length Jane stood upon her feet. In her bosom she felt this was all so terribly wrong. She certainly knew her position in the line of succession as governed by the law of Parliament.

Courageously she collected her wits about her and declared forcefully, "The crown is not my right and pleaseth me not. The Lady Mary is the rightful heir." This denouncement was met with rage by Duddley while her parents derided her as a disobedient daughter. They insisted that such disobedience was against the Lord's commandments and that she should do her duty to her parents and father-in-law. In their presence and upon her knees Jane prayed to God for guidance. She sobbed and cried for help but felt no direction. She mistook this void to mean that despite her dread and fearful reservation she should submit to her parents as the "Scripture sayeth." She stood as if addressing Duddley, her mother and father, the

Council and the Nobles, but in actuality continued her prayer to God.

"If what hath been given to me is lawfully mine, may Thy Divine Majesty grant me such spirit and grace that I may govern to Thy glory and service, and to the advantage of the realm."

So saying she took the throne but in so doing she felt immediately that she had acted without prudence and feared that she had sinned in accepting the title of Queen.

The following day Jane, in royal procession, was escorted to the Palace Apartments in the Tower. She was dressed in an elegant green damask kirtle with a bodice of white and green embroidered in gold. The crown jewels were brought to her and she reluctantly allowed the crown to be fitted to her small head. In the meantime, Duddley had sent his son Robert to capture Mary, whom he knew was the only real threat. Forewarned Mary had fled north where she could garner troops loyal to her and to the Catholic Faith.

On the second day of Queen Jane's reign a great banquet was held in the Tower Palace. It was to herald Duddley's successful intrigue and the preservation of his power. But Mary was far more resilient than he had supposed. She had successfully evaded capture and with temerity had sent a royal dispatch to the Tower which was read aloud at the feast.

"My Lords, we greet you well, and have received sure advertisement that our dearest brother the King is departed to God . . . now after his death, concerning the crown and governance of this realm of England what has been provided by Act of Parliament . . . there is no good true subject that can or will pretend to be ignorant thereof. . . .Wherefore, my lords, we require and charge you . . . [to] cause our right and title to the crown and government of this realm to be proclaimed . . . and this letter signed with our hand shall be your sufficient warrant. Mary"

Profound silence held the hall in astonishment, broken at length by the lamentations of Jane's mother, the Duchess of Suffolk and by the cries of the Duchess of Northumberland, Duddley's wife. While he became torrid in his power mania, Jane showed no emotion whatever and remained silent. Duddley and his fellow councilors assured her that Mary was without support and that she had nothing to fear from this bold declaration. It was now perfectly obvious to Jane what John Duddley had schemed to accomplish. Alone with Guildford, her husband, she informed him that there was no provision in Edward VI's decree that would authorize his becoming king consort—nor would she allow it. He flew into a tantrum and swore he would be king. This had no effect upon Queen Jane who, in absolute composure, flatly stated as ruling monarch that she would never permit his ascension. With this, his courage completely failed him and he ran to his mother sobbing, "I will not be a duke, I will be king." He was about to depart court with his mother when Queen Jane, with far more spunk than anyone had imagined forbade his departure, "I have no need of my husband in bed, but by day his place is at my side."

Jane promised as Queen to be "most benign and gracious to all her people, and to maintain God's holy word and the laws of the land." But alas, her reign was so brief that her radiance was not allowed to warm the hearts of her people or contribute to their welfare and security. History has called her the nine-day queen. How she would have changed history had she ruled for even nine years!

John Duddley knew that he must move quickly to strengthen his position and ignoring Jane's statement, declared that in two weeks both Jane and his son Guildford would be crowned Queen and King. Mary had raised a force at Framlingham Castle that has been estimated by various sources to be from 14,000 to 40,000 men at arms. Most likely her army numbered 20,000. Unaware of her strength, Duddley departed from London with his force of 5,000 soldiers on July 14. Word of Mary's strength began to reach Duddley's army lowering morale and causing many to desert. Furthermore, intelligence relayed to the Council confirmed that Duddley was vastly out manned and out gunned. The Councilors and Noblemen knew they were supporting a lost cause and forgetting the sworn oath to uphold Queen Jane with their own blood quickly turned-coat and changed their allegiance to Mary.

On July 18 all but three councilors left the Tower Palace and, away from Queen Jane at Baynard's Castle, declared that Duddley was guilty of treason against the rightful Queen Mary. They ordered him to dismiss his army and offered a reward of up to 1000 pounds for his capture. Duddley withdrew his men when nearly within sight of Mary's forces when he ascertained for certain how badly outnumbered he was. Many of his men fell to rape, looting and pillaging—Duddley did nothing to restrain them. When on the 20th of July news reached him that Mary had been proclaimed Queen by the Council in London, He fled with those men still in his command to Cambridge to try to arouse the body of students to his lost cause. This effort was totally unsuccessful. He was arrested shortly thereafter cravenly begging for mercy and was taken to the Tower prison to await trial.

In the meantime, on July 19, the silence of the nearly deserted royal apartments of Queen Jane was shattered by her father and Tower officials. Jane was sitting beneath the canopy of estate when he entered abruptly and declared that she was no longer the queen. In a dramatic gesture he tore down the canopy and commanded that she "put off" her "royal robes." With regal dignity, her composure unruffled she calmly responded:

"I much more willingly put them off than I put them on. Out of obedience to you and my mother I have grievously sinned. Now I willingly relinquish the crown. May I go home?"

This he did not permit. He left his daughter in the Tower to await the justice or mercy of Queen Mary, according to her pleasure. Henry Grey was a recreant and was without natural affection. He cravenly forsook his guileless Jane and feigned loyalty to Mary. Had he just returned to his idleness and dissipating amusements Jane may well have found Mary merciful. But no, Henry and Francis Grey could not be content with the power and wealth that came with their titles of Duke and Duchess of Suffolk. We shall see how their ambition would ultimately lead to the scaffold of the Tower. Jane knew that she was under arrest when several hours after her father's departure, guards were posted outside her chambers.

Mary indeed was crowned Queen of England. Jane and Guildford were kept imprisoned in the Tower. Rapidly Mary rolled back the clock restoring the type of monarchy that ruled England before her Father King Henry VIII broke from the Holy Roman Church. The persecution of Catholics ceased and the persecution of Protestants began. Mary's younger sister Elizabeth, as a pretense, converted to Catholicism as did the Council, and most of the Lords and Ladies of the realm. For some, this meant release from prison and pardon from the Queen. Jane, however, never wavered from her convictions and remained very vocal as to her religion. Nevertheless she was humble and regarded herself a loyal subject to Queen Mary. Mary's advisors thought it dangerous to allow a Protestant heir to remain alive and although they all knew that Jane had received her appointment as Queen from the highest officers in the Kingdom without personal aspiration and was more pleased to step down from the throne than she was to step up to it, still, they pressed Mary to execute her. But Jane's sincerity and goodness appealed to Mary who told her advisors that when the time was right, and she felt secure in their release, she would issue Jane and Guildford a pardon and grant them their freedom.

A month passed. John Duddley was tried on August 18 for high treason and was found guilty. The deposed Dictator must die! He pled to Bishop Gardiner that he had seen the error of his ways and wished to convert saying, "I would do penance all the days of my life, if it were but in a mousehole. Is there no hope of mercy?" He was given several days to convert to the Roman Church, and confess his sins. Jane watched from her window in the Tower as her father-in-law was led in solemn procession to St. Peter's to hear Mass. During a conversation around her Gentleman Gaoler's dining table, Jane reflected on this strange sight of the Protestant Lord Protector, formerly the most powerful man in the Kingdom, being led meekly to Mass. Would this act save his life as it had others? Jane's words show clear and accurate thinking and again foreshadow her own fate.

> ". . . though other men be of that opinion (that his conversion would save him), I utterly am not; for what man is there living . . . that would hope of life . . . being in the field against the Queen in person as general [and being] so hated and evil spoken of by the commons . . . Who was judge that he should hope for pardon, whose life was odious to all men? But like as his life was wicked so was his end thereafter . . .
>
> "Should I who am young . . . forsake my faith for the love of life? Nay, God forbid! Much more he should not whose, fatal course, although he had lived his just number of years, could not have long continued. But life is sweet, it appeared. So he might have lived, you will say, he did not care how. . . . But God be merciful to us, for he saith, 'Whoso denyeth him before men, he will not know him in his Father's kingdom.'"

When Duddley was taken to the scaffold and his head placed on the block, he simply said:

> "I have deserved a thousand deaths."

In one blow of the axe his life was ended.

On the November 16, 1553 Jane and Guildford were tried and found guilty of treason, but no date was set for their execution. Jane carved a Latin inscription on the wall of her cell *I hope for light after the darkness*. The months of imprisonment and the death-fruit of his evil father seemed to be changing Guildford into something human. He carved upon his cell wall one simple word *JANE*. A month later the Gaolers received orders to improve the prisoner's quarters and Lady Jane was given the freedom of walking in the Queen's Garden between the inner and outer walls of the Tower. It appeared that light indeed was beginning to break and soon they would be pardoned and set at liberty.

Mary intensified her persecutions. She began to burn Protestants at the stake as heretics. Many of her subjects began to fear that her Spanish blood might compel her to inaugurate the Inquisition in England (Mary's mother Katherine was aunt to Charles V, The Holy Roman Emperor). When Mary announced that she would marry Prince Phillip of Spain, a conspiracy arose to dethrone her. The conspirators were led by Sir Thomas Wyatt and by the end of January 1554 he was General of between four to five thousand men in open rebellion against the Crown. Worst of all he had enlisted the support of the Duke of Suffolk! Henry Grey had agreed to join the rebels with considerable assistance on the condition that Wyatt would depose Mary and set his daughter once again upon the throne! The conspiracy failed, the battles were lost to forces loyal to Mary.

Among the 680 taken prisoner or arrested was found Henry Grey. While his daughter Jane had been locked in the Tower, he had been at liberty nursing his wounded ambition in the hopes of this deadly intrigue. All hope of mercy from Queen Mary was gone. Mary perceived that her leniency had nearly resulted in the loss of her Crown and "blood was necessary to wash away the stain of rebellion." Jane did not want the Crown. She had felt her acceptance of it in the first instance to be a sin of vanity, which she had dearly repented of. She knew nothing of her father's plans and would have disowned his scheme with vehemence had she known. He had betrayed her utterly and completely.

Jane and Guildford were sentenced to be beheaded upon the scaffold of the Tower. Yet her Christlike forgiveness proved that she could not be embittered. She wrote to her father a letter to live through all time.

"Although it hath pleased God to hasten my death by you, by whom my life should rather have been lengthened, yet can I patiently take it, that I yield God more hearty thanks for shortening my woeful days, than if all the world had been given unto my possession, with life lengthened at my own will. . . .yet, my dear father, if I may without offence rejoice in my own mishap, herein I account myself blessed, that washing my hands with the innocency of my face, my guiltless blood may cry before the Lord, 'Mercy to the innocent'...In taking [the crown] upon me, I seemed to consent and therein grievously offended the Queen and her laws...And thus, good father, I have opened unto you the state in which I presently stand, my death at hand, although to you it may seem woeful, yet to me, there is nothing more welcome than from this vale of misery to aspire to that heavenly throne of all joy and pleasure, with Christ our saviour...

Your obedient daughter 'til death

Jane Duddley."

To Queen Mary Jane wrote:

"Although my fault be such that but for the goodness and clemency of the Queen, I can have no hope of finding pardon...having given ear to those who at the time appeared not only to myself, but also to the great part of this realm to be wise and now have manifested themselves to the contrary, not only to my and their great detriment, but with common disgrace and blame of all, they having with shameful boldness made to blamable and dishonorable an attempt to give to others that which was not theirs...[I have shown a] lack of prudence...for which I deserve heavy punishment...it being known that the error imputed to me has not been altogether caused by myself....As to the rest, for my part, I know not what the Council had determined to do, but I know for certain that twice during this time, poison was given to me, first in the house of the Duchess of Northumberland and afterwards here in the Tower... All these I have wished for the witness of my innocence and the disburdening of my conscience."

Mary was once again moved with feelings of clemency. However as long as Jane was Protestant she could not be allowed to live. If she would but convert, and Mary knew that Jane's integrity would allow no pretense, she would pose no threat to her papal kingdom. Who would seek to depose a Catholic Queen to instate another Catholic? She dispatched a priest, one Richard Feckenham, to Jane to attempt to proselytize her into the Holy Roman Church. Feckenham was kindly and was no doubt very much impressed with Lady Jane and did his utmost to, in his estimation, both save her soul and her mortal life.

Jane warmed to the old priest but would not in the least compromise her Faith. After repeated efforts failed, Feckenham required that Jane, with Queen Mary's assent, debate theology with him publicly in one of the chapels in the Tower. Imagine, a sixteen year old girl debating the weightiest matters of religion with a learned scholar with such age and status that he was counselor to Queen Mary! Jane far more than held her own. The priest saw there was no hope of success with Jane and said, "Madam, I am sorry for you for I am now sure that we shall never meet [in the hereafter]."

Jane responded sincerely and with fervor.

"It is true, Sir, we never shall meet, except God turn your heart; for I am assured, unless you repent and turn to God, you are in a sad and desperate case; and I pray God, of his infinite mercy, to send you his Holy Spirit; for he hath given you his great gift of utterance, if it pleases him also to open your heart."

What courage! Declaring that he was "in a sad and desperate case" when she was the one sentenced to death! On the eve of her death, February 11, 1554 Jane wrote the following:

"If justice is done with my body, my soul will find mercy with God. Death will give pain to my body for its sins, but the soul will be justified before God. If my faults deserve punishment, my youth at least, and my imprudence were worthy of excuse. God and posterity will show me more favor."

The following morning Guildford was led first to the scaffold. He had the courage to ask for a Protestant Priest but was denied such comfort. He spoke with his friends, shook hands and knelt in prayer. He had sent Jane notice of his love for her the day before and had received words of comfort back from her. How his suffering and foreknowledge of death had strengthened him—whereas the same fate had reduced his father to absolute ruin! Jane had witnessed Guildford's rise in character and now regarded him as her worthy husband and hoped that they would not only meet in Heaven, but unite there eternally.

Every person must face the moment of death and now Guildford's time had come. A few short months earlier his father, John Duddley, met this crisis in great shame on the same scaffold without faith of redemption. Although they both met the same end, the guilty father died a hopeless wicked wretch while the innocent son died at the summit of his goodness, in the faith of his Lord and his wife Jane. As Guildford laid his head upon the block his final words were, "Pray for me! Pray for me!"

The cart carrying his headless body wrapped in a bloody sheet was wheeled past Jane's apartment and at the sight of it she recoiled in horror. And then she sobbed, "O Guilford! Guilford! O the bitterness of death!" Now would she remain faithful? Could she endure steadfast to the very end—for the end of life now stared mightily upon her and what had been courageous words now must be proven in very deed. Clemency was still hers if she denied her faith. With all the strength of her soul she prayed.

"[Let] me not deny Thee, my God. Be unto me a strong tower of defense. Suffer me not to be tempted above my power, I beseech Thee that I may stand fast."

On the arm of Sir John Bridges, who wept mournfully and manfully, she was led to Tower Green. But Jane was calm, full of the Spirit of God. As she walked, she read from her little prayer book. When mounting the scaffold, she turned to the nobles who were gathered to bear witness of her execution.

"Good people, I am come hither to die, and by a law I am condemned to the same. The fact, indeed, against the Queen's Highness was unlawful, and the consenting thereunto by me: but touching the procurement and desire thereof by me, I do wash my hands in innonceny before God and the face of you, good Christian people. I pray you all to bear me witness that I die a true Christian woman. And now, good people, while I am alive, I pray you assist me with your prayers."

She asked the Abbot Feckenham if she could read the 51st Psalm and he could scarce utter yes, so choked he was with emotion. She read as an angel:

"Have mercy upon me, O God, according to thy loving kindness: according unto the multitude of thy tender mercies blot out my transgressions.

Wash me throughly from mine iniquity, and cleanse me from my sin.

For I acknowledge my transgressions: and my sin [is] ever before me.

Against thee, thee only, have I sinned, and done [this] evil in thy sight: that thou mightest be justified when thou speakest, [and] be clear when thou judgest.

Purge me with hyssop, and I shall be clean: wash me, and I shall be whiter than snow.

Make me to hear joy and gladness; [that] the bones [which] thou hast broken may rejoice.

Hide thy face from my sins, and blot out all mine iniquities.

Create in me a clean heart, O God; and renew a right spirit within me.

Cast me not away from thy presence; and take not thy holy spirit from me.

Restore unto me the joy of thy salvation; and uphold me [with thy] free spirit.

[Then] will I teach transgressors thy ways; and sinners shall be converted unto thee.

Deliver me from bloodguiltiness, O God, thou God of my salvation: [and] my tongue shall sing aloud of thy righteousness.

O Lord, open thou my lips; and my mouth shall shew forth thy praise."

She held Abbot Feckenham's hand and bid him a final Adieu saying, "God I beseech Him abundantly reward you for your kindness towards me." She recognized his attempts to convert her were done in the charity of his heart, but she added, "Although I must needs say it was more unwelcome to me than my instant death is terrible." Her final testament that conversion *away* from her faith would be far worse to her than death itself!

Jane removed her gloves and gave them to her lady Mrs. Tilney and her prayer book to Sir John Bridges. Then she untied her outer gown. She received from another attendant, Mrs. Ellen, a scarf to blindfold herself. The executioner knelt at her feet and asked her forgiveness which "she gave willingly." Then she said to him, "I pray you will dispatch me quickly." What followed was a most pitiful sight—beautiful Jane, hallowed Jane, blindfolded, could not find the block. She cried as a lost lamb, "What shall I do? Where is it?" As when she cried in Syon house, no one would help her and she groped blindly trying to find the terrible pillow where she would rest her head for the last time. But this was different—who could help her to hasten her death?—she had held them all spellbound with her eloquence and spirituality. At last a person who will forever be unknown took her hands and guided them to the wine colored block, still wet with her husband's blood. With perfect composure she prayed, "Lord, into Thy hands I commend my spirit." So ended her mortal life. So began her immortal life—to be made Eternal in the morning of the resurrection of the just!

Queen Jane was yet in the springtime of her life when she died an innocent martyr for truth. If all there was of her life were sixteen years and no more, her brilliance snuffed out of existence long before the zenith of her career, her ending would be a tragedy without hope of comfort. Lord Macaulay's lamentation that there is so sadder spot on the earth would then be justified. But is such a death so immersed in distress? Or is her mortal end such a triumphant victory that our tears are not wet with sorrow, but are expressions of unspeakable joy? Weep according to your own judgement! The Truth cares not for our opinions and stands independent in its own sphere. God does not create genius, integrity, kindness, goodness, faithfulness, endurance and love, to be stamped out of existence by the whim of mortal man or woman. In short, God did not create Jane to live but sixteen years, regardless of an earthly queen's death decree. The moment the axe descended, Jane was beyond death, beyond suffering and beyond pain. She was far removed from the "vale of misery," the valley of evil intrigue that had so long engulfed her in its evil shadows. She had entered the life of "immortal felicity." The eternal happiness that she had written of in faith, she now experienced personally. At the moment of Jane's death her faith became knowledge. All of the Christ-like attributes of intelligence and charity that Jane had acquired through diligent effort were still hers to enjoy but became tremendously magnified by her birth into immortality. In her temporal life she had completed her life's mission. She accomplished the purpose of her birth.

Ben Jonson wrote:

It is not growing like a tree
In bulk, doth make man better be;
Or standing long an oak, three hundred year,
To fall a log at last, dry, bald, and sere;
   The lily of the day,
   Is fairer far in May,
Although it fall and die that night;
It was the plant and flower of Light.
In small proportions we just beauties see;
And in short measures, life may perfect be.

Through determined acts of self-control, Jane had conquered all of her foes in her short battle of life. Is it a better thing to so triumph in a long drawn-out war of many years? Life is a battle. Its purpose is to prove us. Is one more blessed because his or her period of testing lasts 80 years instead of a brief 16? Jane was surrounded, even in her own family, by her enemies. Hester Chapman in her biography of Jane Grey entitles one chapter "The Sale of Lady Jane." The names Henry and Frances Grey will forever be names of infamy—parents who sold their souls for 2,000 pounds when they sold their daughter as a ward. Jane defeated the Duke and Duchess while honoring in righteousness their title as father and mother. In fact, her virtuous life brought the only honor to their otherwise ignominious existences. Jane defeated the traitorous Lord High Admiral, Thomas Seymour, her guardian. She defeated the murderous Dictator, John Dudley, her father-in-law. And above all, she defeated Queen Mary. Jane had said that if her own generation dealt harshly with her, future generations would be more kind. Her prophecy has been realized more fully than she could possibly have imagined. One of the highest compliments that can be given to any girl or woman is to have appended to her name the title "Lady." It is a rank of exalted nobility. It denotes virtue, goodness, exquisite manners, faithfulness. This tribute to Queen Jane is entitled "Lady Jane"—for so she is! The epithet by which her executioner, Queen Mary, is known by posterity brings horribly to mind her reign of inquisition where hundreds were murdered by flame and axe. We know her as "Bloody Mary!"

You will recall that when Ascham found Jane reading instead of taking her pleasure in the park, hunting with her parents, he was astounded to find that she was occupied with Plato's *Phaedo*. This dialogue is set in the prison of Socrates and is incident to his death. It was Jane's favorite work, outside of Scripture. Jane loved to compare the inspired words found in the Classics with the absolute revealed truth found in God's Word, especially regarding the soul's survival after death and the potential for salvation in the next world. In *Phaedo* Socrates states:

> "If the soul is really immortal, what care should be taken of her, not only in respect of the portion of time which is called life, but of eternity! . . . If death had only been the end of all, the wicked would have had a good bargain in dying, for they would have been happily [rid] not only of their body, but of their own evil . . . But now, as the soul [is] immortal, there is no release or salvation from evil except the attainment of the highest virtue and wisdom. For the soul when on her progress [beyond mortal death] takes nothing with her but nurture and education . . . at the very beginning of its pilgrimage in the other world. . . . I ought to be grieved at death if I were not persuaded that I am going to [God] . . . and therefore I do not grieve . . . The [student of truth] has reason to be of good cheer when he is about to die . . . After death he will be able to obtain the greatest good in the other world . . . **When I come to the end of my journey I shall obtain that which has been the pursuit of my life.**"

Bibliography

Primary Sources

Weir, Alison: *The Children of Henry VIII* (Ballantine Books, New York)

Chapman, Hester: *Lady Jane Grey* (Pan Books LTD: London)

Falkus, Christopher: *The Private Lives Of The Tudor Monarchs* (London: The Folio Society)

Fox, John: *Fox's Book of Martyrs, Chapter XVI*

Wilson, Derek: *The Tower, The Tumultuous History of The Tower of London From 1078* (Charles Scribner's Sons, New York)

Plato: *Phaedo* (Harvard Classics Volume 2)

The Bible

The Girl with Many Names

Irena—Iruska—Rachel—Irene—Mala—Sonia

Perhaps when we left our heavenly home to fulfill our divinely appointed mission here on earth we were known by a name we've long since forgotten. At birth we received what is called our *given name* by which we are normally called throughout life. After death, in the world to come, we may yet be given another name that will be ours through eternity. In this progression we are the same person, but with each name comes a new level of experience. Each experience is like a totally different life, yet it is the same life in the process of maturing—from pre-mortal to mortal to eternal. There are those, here and now, who are given a new name—a life saving name; often without realizing it they are given a new heaven-sent purpose. Their past seems like a distant dream and like another life.

> "The town seemed peaceful and quiet, except for the intermittent chirping of little sparrows, and the greetings from a few farm dogs as we passed by. Breathing freely in the cold, nippy air, I pondered my new identity. I was toasty warm, bundled in an oversized, winter coat that Meriam had found for me. It seemed to me that I really *was* Rachel Mayier, and that my memories were events that had happened in the life of another person."

This is the story of Irena, Iruska, Rachel, Irene, Mala, and Sonia. Each name is a life, but it is the same life of the same girl from Poland—and to each name was given a purpose from God.

Irena Gut was born on the 5th of May, 1922, in the picturesque village of Kozienice in eastern Poland. She was the eldest daughter of a young architect, Wladyslaw Gut and his wife, Maria. Maria was an extraordinary mother endowed with that intuitive sense that exceptional mothers possess. As the mother of the unborn babe sees and feels for the life within her womb, so it is that after birth such mothers continue to see beyond their child's sight and feel beyond their child's grasp. Maria, fondly called Mamusia, knew that Irena possessed a God-given destiny of great import. Mamusia relayed the story to her again and again of how Heavenly Father had saved her life when she was a toddler. It was springtime; the river just below their home was swollen from the melting snows. The laughing sound of the white-capped water through the open window enticed Irena to go exploring. She obviously had been born with the spirit of adventure! While her mother was distracted by household chores, tiny Irena toddled from the home, across the fresh grass of spring, to the beckoning river. The family dog, Myszka, dutifully trotted beside the tottering child. As Maria swayed precariously at the very brink, her tiny shadow cast on the swirling and rumbling white water, Myszka bit down into the diaper of the baby and started backing her away. Irena tried crawling forward, but the determined dog held firm. Dazzled by the sparkling river, the stubborn child, over the next minutes, worked to overcome the opposition of the little dog, gradually creeping closer. Then that voice which silently whispers in the hearts of mothers caused Mamusia to look from the window. "Irena!" She rushed out, snatching her child from the very edge of the torrent. Maszka, exhausted, sank to the ground as the grateful mother praised her.

Myszka became a local hero, praised by the villagers and proclaimed as such in the headlines of the town paper. But her mother saw their little dog as an instrument of a higher power. She would always conclude the telling of her story with: "God saved your life, my dear daughter, for a reason. He has something special in mind for you."

Certainly our faith in ourselves and our sense of purpose in life increases in proportion to that faith and trust our loved ones show in us. Irena was inspired by her mother's presentiments and felt truly she was put on the earth for a righteous cause. Her premonitions were further reinforced through an old holiday custom. At Christmastime Grandmother Rebies would gather the girls around the stove to melt candle wax. Then each girl would pour some of the wax into ice cold water—instantly solidifying the glob into a fortune telling composition. They would hold their enigmatic creation up to the light and analyze its shadow. Irena's looked like a ship upon the sea and from its prow a crucifix. All felt that this signified that Irena was destined for a life of righteous adventure.

Maria and Wladyslaw were dearly and deeply in love and this love blessed their marriage and home with wonderful harmony. They taught Irena and her four younger sisters that happiness was joy earned through faith, service, work, and love for all life. Children naturally love living things until they are taught otherwise or unless they are not given the early opportunity to discover the wonders of creation. In the Gut home the inherent natural affections of the girls together with their innate sympathies were nurtured by Maria. The girls and their mother had especially tender feelings for animals. They lavished affection upon wounded cats, dogs, birds; any creature that was afflicted became a part of the household. Mamusia's care was expert and their home became a sanctuary. One baby blackbird, that had fallen injured from its nest, was healed and raised by Mamusia. When it was well and turned free, it nonetheless always stayed close by their home. When Mamusia would whistle, it would return to her, flying through an open window. Not all of the injured animals could be healed, even with Mamusia's nursing. Those who died were lovingly buried in the backyard.

In such a home Irena grew into a young woman of compassion and empathy. She had been raised to be protective of that which was weaker than herself and possessed a talent of caring for the ill and a yearning to become a greater healer. In her mid-teens she became a Red Cross volunteer and in 1938, at the age of 16, left her family to enter nursing school in Radom. Irena loved to learn and immersed herself in her studies. When the other student nurses left the dormitory to socialize in the evenings, Irena was happy for the quiet hours that followed and would use them to her full advantage. However, she was anything but a wallflower and could have filled her nights with youthful romance. Irena was simply beautiful—blonde hair, blue eyes, striking features, crowned with a sparkling intellect and a persona of kindness. Such Aryan features and attributes would prove to be both her sorrow and her salvation.

Many of us have suffered trauma from a sudden shock—an unexpected violent upheaval. We may have experienced something such as a terrible automobile crash or lived through the devastation of an earthquake; we may have lost the love of our bosom or have just been told that we have a terminal cancer. Possibilities are numerous, but at such times we are thrust from our comfortable world of security into a new world of chaos. In the aftermath we are dazed, dumbfounded. We know that it is still our life that we are living but it is so foreign—so completely detached from our former life that we can scarce believe the new reality. The new experience is to us a new existence. In anguish so many have cried their remonstrance to the heavens, often in a single word containing a single syllable: "Why?" And so often the answer cannot be understood (no matter how hard we try) in the present life or in the experience then in progress. Mortal life is designed to teach us truths that are eternal in nature and forge godly attributes in our souls that we will possess forever! Sometimes we only truly and lastingly learn from trauma.

However difficult our lives are in such circumstances, only those who have experienced *Blitzkrieg* can say that they know what Irena felt on September 1, 1939. After a thoroughly enjoyable first year and a delightful summer vacation with her family, Irena entered her second year at nursing school. It was a clear, warm day; the first bright sunny day after a spell of steady rain. Irena, walking to the hospital, suddenly heard the drone of aircraft engines, followed by the deafening roar of explosions. The blue skis of Radom were blackened by row upon row of bombers—German bombers flying in formation. At that moment, the earth beneath Irene's feet shook from bomb blasts. Before her very eyes the wall of a building directly across the street crumbled away revealing the furnished apartments within. It now stood like a surreal doll's house.

Irena, shocked by the horror, was unable to think or move. She did not know where to run and so she just stood, stunned, as billows of smoke rose all around her. Sirens wailed as the screams of more bombs filled the air; blast upon blast in every direction! Radom had suddenly become one huge, searing torch! The panic stricken inhabitants ran in every direction; parents screamed for children, the cries of the brutally injured added to the growing pitch of hysteria. One little naked child sat sobbing upon a doorstep; behind him nothing—his home instantly gone. The scene was of sheer madness which increased with every pulsating moment.

Irena would have probably been killed in that instant had not a hospital intern dragged her into a ditch. Although debris rained down upon their heads and Irena was cut from flying masonry, they were otherwise unharmed. The days that followed were endless for Irena who worked around the clock at St. Mary Hospital along with every available hand. Overflowing with wounded, a hospital bed became a luxury. The sufferers were everywhere—on the floors, in the hallways and on the stairways. The priests, administering the last rites to the dead, were as busy as the doctors and nurses. It was impossible to know if her family was still alive and there was no way to go to them.

While the German ground divisions, the lightning war machine, rolled ever closer to Radom, the Polish Army was forced to rapidly retreat. As their forces hastily pulled out of Radom an officer asked for volunteers from the medical staff to accompany them. Without hesitation Irena raised her hand. There was no time to even pack a suitcase.

All she had were the clothes on her back as she stepped from the hospital. For the past four days she had only seen the injured, the dead and dying inside. It was a shock for Irena to see blue sky, the warm sun and clouds lightly billowing. As she climbed into a Red Cross ambulance filled with injured soldiers, Irena wondered how—with her beloved Poland being brutally murdered—how could the sun still shine?

The roads were in complete pandemonium—a terrible runoff from the flash flood of war. Every possible highway and byway overrun with evacuees. The Nazi advance was so rapid that there was no time for the appallingly outgunned Polish Army to regroup and counter the offensive. Despite the frenzy, Irena's unit arrived at a train station where by rail they could more swiftly retreat to meet with reinforcements. They would go east northeast towards Kovno and Russia. As Irena was assisting the wounded board the train, suddenly the sound of aircraft filled the air with horror. Incendiary bombs fell from the sky. Irena felt the burning heat steal the oxygen from the air. At the same moment the roof of the train station and trees that lined the tracks burst into flame. She could not even fill her lungs enough to scream. Incredibly, she helped another nurse push a wounded soldier into a carriage. A moment later the train lurched forward—the noise of its engine drowned out by the din of the German bombardment and the piercing cries of the dying.

The journey to Kovno was a long one and while traveling they were cut off from all news of the war. When they arrived, they learned that Poland was no more—their country had been divided between the Germans and the Soviets. The Polish Army had formally ceased to exist except in small leaderless remnants. Irena had no possible means to return home and could not know if home still existed. Consequently, she stayed with her "ragtag army-without-a-country." There was no real commander and no organization. All were zealous and patriotic but lacked even basic equipment, such as tents and coats. To surrender to the Russians would mean incarceration as prisoners of war so they lived in the forest and did their best to barter for food with villagers. They had left fall weather in the south for winter cold in Kovno. Now, they tried to work their way southward to Lvov, some 500 kilometers away. Without shelter, sufficient food, and winter clothing, most became sick. Irena also became very weak, barely surviving. After four months their group was finally near

Lvov. They were an army without purpose, with no means of retreat or refuge.

One night in January Irena went into a small town to try and barter for some essentials. Suddenly she heard the sound of a truck and before she could hide, she was caught in its headlights. She fled as fast as her malnourished legs could carry her towards the forest. The Russian soldiers had no difficulty running her down in the snow. She pled for mercy but there was no humanity left in these wolves. She struggled and was beaten senseless. They laughed as they tore her clothing and her body. Irena, who had never even kissed a boy, was raped, brutalized and left in blood stained snow to die. Impossible as it seems, on that dark winter night, another patrol found her. She awoke in a warm hospital bed miles away in Ternopol. Her wounds had been carefully dressed.

When she was capable of speaking, Irena was questioned by a Russian woman, Dr. Olga, chief of staff of the Ternopol Hospital. Irena told how she had been stranded by the war, had scavenged for food in the forest like an animal and had been viscously molested by the soldiers. Dr. Olga was well aware of this last humiliation. It was she who had treated her, not as a prisoner of war, which in fact she was, but had carefully tended the wounds of this nearly frozen patient. Dr. Olga's voice was kind but her appearance was severe. Irena wanted to believe that her apparent benefactor was good and noble. Was she as kind as her soft words or was she as dark as her countenance? It seemed the former was true, for after she recovered she was not sent to a P.O.W. camp. Dr. Olga had her move into the nurse's dormitory and her skills were once again put to use. Irena's name was Russianized and she was now called Iruska. Her new life required a new language. A nurse named Maruszka, a girl near her age, took her under her wing and taught her grammar. The chief of surgery, Dr. David, was sensitive to Iruska and she soon felt drawn to him. Her skills rapidly improved, both in terms of her medical expertise and in her ability to communicate with the Soviets. As a "prisoner" she was restricted completely to the hospital, which was fenced and under guard—but she was working, regaining her health, serving the afflicted and was learning. Therefore she was becoming happy again.

Dr. Olga would at times single out Iruska from the other nurses, complementing her on her Russian or her proficiency at her job. At these moments she could feel the other girls stare at her. Were they jealous or was there another meaning to their glares? By now she was better physically than she had been in seven months. The sheen had returned to her golden hair, which when let down, fell softly upon her shoulders. The almost manly Dr. Olga had even pronounced Iruska "beautiful" and favored her as her companion for dinner. Although she had been through the horrors of war, the seventeen year old girl from Poland was still naïve. However, after repeated attentions that were unnatural in character, Iruska had a terrible nightmare. It was horrible and she willed herself to wake up, but could not—her sleep was so heavy. The dreadfulness of her dream centered around Dr. Olga. When she awoke she felt bruised and very confused. Nonetheless, when she became immersed in the normalcy of her work she shook off her growing dread of the doctor and dismissed her fears as childish. Then one evening Dr. Olga invited her again to supper. As they dined she explained that she was about to be transferred to Moscow and wanted her to come and live with her. This by itself could have been an offer of freedom from her prisoner of war status. However, Dr. Olga continued with her scheme, with an innuendo that was revolting, telling Iruska that men are coarse, brutal and merciless—while women are kind, gentle and empathetic. "Trust me, my sweet little one," she whispered.

Now the light dawned completely in Iruska's mind. She knew she had been drugged before by this perverse wretch—a demon in reality. It was not just a nightmare! Even as she resolutely refused the awful proposition she felt herself being drawn once again into the blackness of oblivion. It was a long while before she regained consciousness.

When she awakened, Dr. David was there. He explained to Iruska that Dr. Olga had informed him she had been treating Iruska for an illness. Olga claimed that the young nurse had suffered a violent reaction to medication she had been given and had lapsed into unconsciousness. She said she had to leave immediately for her new post in Moscow and told him to continue treatment. Dr. David looked at her sympathetically, "You gave us quite a scare, Iruska." Oh, how she wanted to tell him the truth but she was so ashamed and filled with self-loathing. Now she knew why the other nurses acted the way they did when they saw her with Olga—and it was certainly not a matter of envy. This time the outward signs of abuse were minimal but she knew that she had been violated and had been nearly murdered. How she needed consolation! How Iruska needed someone who would tell her that a girl sexually victimized is not the sinner—that a mongrel dog cannot steal virtue—that she was still clean and holy before God! How she needed a true friend and how she prayed for such an ally and for deliverance from this hellish prison called a hospital. Her prayers were answered and she was given a friend in the person of Dr. David. But she was not to know this for sure until after one more ordeal.

The new chief of staff was Dr. Ksydzof, a vulger man whose eyes followed her whenever they were in the same room. Now she knew well what a certain gaze meant! How dark eyes, eyes without light, are the portals to a dead soul. She avoided him as much as she possibly could. She had learned that it was not her skill as a nurse that had been her ticket to such a comfortable life style in a time of awful war. Polish doctors and nurses were indeed used by the Russians—to care for those with deadly contagions such as the bubonic plague—they were expendable. No, Olga had favored Iruska because of her beauty which she lusted after, as did Dr. Ksydozof. Her beauty was indeed her deliverance and her distress.

One night she retired alone to her bedroom. Her roommates were having a loud party next door. She turned out the lights and wearily slipped under her covers and immediately fell asleep. Suddenly there was the smell of liquor and the awful smothering of someone crushing her under his mass. A crude warning hissed from Dr. Ksydozof's mouth, "Don't make a sound—you are mine now!" Not again—please God, not again! He seized her right wrist as she struggled with all of her might, but her left hand caught hold of a milk bottle filled with cold tea. Down went the bottle upon his head with a crack and instantly he was dead weight. She fled in her nightclothes down the hallway and down the stairs to Dr. David. He did his best to calm her. Then he left her in the comparative safety of an examination room while he went to investigate. He found her room vacant! She had not killed Ksydozof but Dr. David knew as did Iruska, that she must escape and escape soon. Not many days later Iruska's slender figure slipped through a loose board in the hospital fence, on her person was a train ticket for Swietlana, a gift of life from Dr. David. In this small village near Kiev Dr. David had a friend, a woman who ran the town infirmary. She had answered his plea to provide safe haven for Iruska. As she fled for her life she knew that Dr. David had risked his own to save hers.

There are fiends in this world, "whited sepulchers," who look human on the outside but within are death and misery. The Russian soldiers who had ravished Iruska, along with Olga and Ksydozof, had joined the fallen race of devils. They had once been created in the image of God but now in their depravity they bore the image of their adopted father—he who had fallen in the beginning. All of this poor girl's suffering to this point in her life was but an inoculation for the epidemic that was spreading the disease of war around the world. The loathsome center of the infection was in her country and growing ever more deadly. She would yet face horrors that would make these past crimes pale in comparison.

There are also saints in this world! Born in the image of their Creator they not only retain their humanity but through charity, which is pure godly love, become increasingly more like their Father in Heaven. These follow the opposite path and choose to assimilate divinity instead of deviltry. Such were Dr. David and Miriam.

The train slowly came to a stop. Iruska opened the door of her compartment and, stepping onto the railway platform, she heard, "Rachel! It's me, Meriam!" She felt herself being embraced from behind and turned to see a dark haired young woman wrapped in a shawl. Before Iruska could speak, Miriam loudly commented on how good it was to see her young *cousin* and how much she had grown. Then taking her arm, and reassuring her that they would soon be home where she could rest after the long journey, Miriam nodded to the ticket agent, "Goodnight, Comrade."

Iruska had become Rachel and along with her new identity would lead a new life, and for a while, a happy one. Often, in the middle of awful tribulation, God grants a temporary reprieve—a time to rebuild one's strength and one's faith. We may think our trials are over when in truth there are far greater battles still to fight. Swietlana was an oasis for Rachel in the scorching desert of war. Dr. Meriam was the antithesis of Dr. Olga. She was genuinely good, benignant and was very lovely. Yet she was efficient, intelligent, a skilled general practitioner who truly provided *care* to the people of the village—often refusing compensation. Rachel assisted Meriam in setting bones, giving vaccinations, stitching wounds, pulling teeth, and caring for the ill. Midwives generally delivered babies unless complications arose—then they would send for Dr. Meriam and her nurse Rachel. Their days were filled with work, the best work—that of helping others. Rachel felt safe and knew she was needed. For the first time in a long time she felt true joy.

Meriam was beloved in Swietlana and was in fact loved by the town magistrate who hoped to woo her into marriage. Soon after her arrival, Rachel noticed that she too was held in this same high regard. She was treated with respect and admiration by the villagers. In the summer of 1940 Rachel willingly exposed herself to typhoid fever to care for a family stricken with the life threatening disease. For six weeks she and Meriam were quarantined with them in three primitive huts on the outskirts of town. The grandfather and mother died of the fever, but their stronger children and their grandchildren survived. The ghastly disease was checked and a possible outbreak prevented. When it was finally safe to return to their infirmary they were greeted by grateful neighbors with gifts such as they had to give—vegetables, fruits, and chickens. On another occasion, a midwife saw that her patient was about to deliver breech. Quickly Dr. Meriam was summoned and successfully brought the child into the world. It was the first birth the 18 year old nurse had ever witnessed. She exclaimed to her benefactor and mentor that she had witnessed a miracle and was transformed by love.

The following January they received a letter from Dr. David in Ternopol that filled Rachel with the hope of reunion with her family. It read:

"The Germans and Russians have agreed to allow Poles who were separated from their families by the invasion, to cross the battle lines in the spring. *If you know of anyone in that situation, you should tell him or her, to go to Ternopol, when the time comes, for processing.*"

Rachel had now lived in peace, far from war's devastation, for twelve months. The awful afflictions she had borne seemed so distant and, although she was truly happy living and working with Meriam, she needed desperately to know of her family's welfare. How she missed them and longed to be reunited! Meriam tried to reason with her. Ternopol was the very place from which she had fled as a fugitive only a year before. Prior to her escape from the hospital she was known to have been a member of a faction of the illegal Polish Army. If she were caught she could endanger the lives of Dr. David and Meriam herself. But Rachel was so determined. After all Dr. David had sent the letter and he must believe that she would want to try and would most likely succeed. When Meriam bid her adopted cousin Rachel a tearful goodbye she admonished her, "I wish I could persuade you to stay here, where you are safe, but I know that is impossible. Keep your wits about you at the border. Anything can happen."

Rachel found that it was a far easier thing to travel to Ternopol than to leave Ternopol. When she arrived she found lines of people, stretched for blocks, Poles who had been waiting for days to be "processed" for repatriation to their homeland. She feared the worst. But once again her blonde hair and blue eyes directed her destiny. There were both Russian and German officers at the gate that allowed entrance to where train tickets could be purchased. A German Lieutenant smiled at her and said, *"Guten Tag, Fräulein"* and authorized her immediate passage. In a short time she held a ticket in her hand for Radom! Fearful lest she might lose this most precious piece of paper she hid it in her brassier. She couldn't believe it—it was one o'clock in the afternoon and her train was scheduled to leave at four a.m. the next morning. I have hours to kill, she thought to herself. That was where she made her mistake.

She strolled down the streets past shops, now nearly empty. She walked through the park, then dined at a little café. It was as she started back towards the park that Rachel was recognized as Iruska by two Russian soldiers and arrested. She was taken to a detention center and interrogated again and again. "What subversive organization are you with now? Where is your gun? Who are your connections? How did you escape from Ternopol Hospital? Where did you go? How did you live? How are you plotting against the U.S.S.R.?" They would leave her to fall asleep in her tiny cell, just to awaken her and once again begin the same line of questioning. She tried to pray but her mind could not form thoughts. She was searched and her purse emptied. But they did not have her remove clothing and her ticket remained safe. This continued all through the night. With the coming of dawn she knew she had missed her train. The Commissar continued his interrogatories at regular intervals throughout the day. Most of what she told him was true—how she had been raped by the Russian soldiers and how Dr. Ksydzof had attempted the same crime. This, she said, was why she had fled. In all that she confessed she said nothing that would incriminate Dr. David or Dr. Meriam.

It was dark outside when she was questioned for the last time. The Commissar seemed to have changed his attitude or at least his approach. He told her that she was young and pretty and he wanted to help. During this entire ordeal she had not eaten and was famished. He gave her tea and bread. He asked if she knew someone in the area with whom she could spend the night. She lied and told him she did. He arranged to have a young Ukrainian guard escort her there, extracting a promise that she return by 8:00 a.m. the following morning. If she did not return exactly at the appointed time she would be in far more serious trouble. Had he really softened towards her or was he hoping that she would lead him to her confederates?

It was well after curfew and the moonlit streets were empty as she walked with the young soldier to where?—she had no idea. It was all a bluff of course. She knew very little of Ternopol. The Ukrainian seemed to enjoy her company more than his mission which, most likely, was to simply see where she would spend the night. Arbitrarily she wound her way through the city hoping to see something that would suggest a plan. At length he asked if she really knew where she was going. She responded by saying that she certainly did but had to get there along the route in which she was familiar. He must have laughed to himself how a simple girl did not possess the internal compass of a soldier.

Then she suddenly saw the answer to her prayers; it was a building on the next street corner. There was a fence along one side which was missing a couple of slats. Irena turned to the soldier, thanking him for the escort and shaking his hand. Then she stood in front of the three story building and watched him round the corner. When he had disappeared, she ran to the space in the fence, squeezed through and ran free.

Irena put as much distance between herself and the corner building as quickly as she could. We will never know the motives of the Commissar— why he released her. We will never know if that night, or when she missed her morning appointment, the building was raided. Certainly the Soviet official did not suspect that she would try the train station. They did not know she had a ticket and would suppose that if she tried to obtain one they would easily apprehend her in the long lines or at the gate. She in fact did have a ticket, hidden as we have said, for a train that was to depart the morning after her arrival. That seemed so long ago! Irena was filled with anxiety; what would she do? She was lost. She could not just knock on a door and ask directions. Would anyone even open their door to her after curfew? If they did, would they help her or betray her to the communists?

She prayed for a miracle and a miracle was exactly what God gave her. As she ran down the streets of Ternopol, she came across a kindly old

Polish man making a trip to the outdoor privy. She surprised him by her sudden appearance and had nothing to lose now that he had seen her. Quickly she pled with him, "Where is the train station?" He was no informer and recognizing her plight, gave her the needed directions. Later that night she arrived wearily at Ternopol Train Station. Nothing had changed. People were everywhere. She pushed her way through the crowd to a German officer and told him that she had been ill and had missed her train. Being alone, with no luggage, she did not know what to do. The young officer looked at her transport card and told her that luckily, because of mechanical trouble, her train had not been able to depart. She had not missed it after all!

In a quiet corner of the depot she knelt and gave thanks to God. When it came time for her 8:00 a.m. appointment with the Commissar she was already three hours down the line heading for Radom! She rode, not in a coach, but in a cattle car, crammed and standing with the rest of the passengers. But it did not matter—she was going home.

Irena peeked through the slats, watching for glimpses of her native land. Spring had come, the woodlands, villages and fields were all freshly dipped in vivid greens. With delight, she noticed that lilacs, her favorite flower, were budding—ready to burst into sweet, soft lavender in time for her birthday, May 5. Now all these reminders stirred up beautiful memories of her idyllic past; a time when Irena's world was filled with peace.

At length, Radom's skyline appeared. Somehow the green of the countryside had lulled Irena into the past and she was shocked to see that there were ruins everywhere—the awful wake of the Blitzkrieg. Suddenly, the joy which had been building inside Irena began to fade as she saw the vast destruction of the city. She hoped that somehow Aunt Helen would still be in Radom and would know the whereabouts of her parents.

It had been nearly two years since Irena's hasty departure with the Polish Army from Radom. Everything had changed including the names of the streets. These new labels were an affront to the love she bore her beloved Poland—names like *Hermann Goring Strasse*. The skeletal remains of buildings were the only remnants of once familiar landmarks. She was completely overcome and lost. Suddenly she felt a genial hand upon her shoulder. She turned and looked into the quiescent eyes of an older Polish gentleman. He said to her that she looked bewildered and offered to take her wherever she needed to go in his horse drawn buggy. She explained that she had no money to pay him. He simply responded that payment was not necessary and as an afterthought mused that she was about the same age as his own daughter, Zofia. He knew his way through the city by the old names and in no time he reigned his horses down the street that led to her Aunt Helen's home. Excitedly Irena recognized houses of old friends. Then to her absolute delight she saw her Aunt's house still standing. She gave the magnanimous driver a quick hug and a kiss on the cheek and flew from his buggy.

There at the gate stood a young girl. Irena did not recognize the pretty, black-haired youth. For a moment, the two stared at each other. Suddenly the girl turned, running into the house hollering, "Irena! Irena!" Instantly, the door was flung open and in the doorway stood her beloved parents! Behind them was her sister, Maria. The young girl was little Bronia.

Irena had survived life-threatening peril when she escaped the Blitzkrieg in Radom with the retreating Polish Army. She had survived the bitter cold of winter living in the forest without protective clothing or shelter. Somehow she clung to life after the brutal attack by the Russians. Twice she had escaped incarceration at Ternopol. She had traveled many hundreds of kilometers by train, truck and on foot with little or no money, led by faith and surviving by her wits. She knew these were indeed miracles—but not as miraculous as finding, in this hellish time of war, her entire family intact and well. Irena writes in her biography:

> "Tell me the happiest you have ever been, and I can say that on that day, I was happier."

Imagine that tender scene of reunion; tears of joy, embraces, laughter, expressions of love, gratitude for each other and to God above! The Gut family was blessed with élan, with the love of life! Gone was their beautiful and spacious home in Kozlowa Gora. Gone were their fine clothes, furnishings, and possessions. Gone were their cherished photographs of family and friends. Gone were their beloved books. All the material goods which make up a house were gone. However, they were blessed, because all that makes up a home remained—Father, Mother, children—all joyously together again.

When the younger sisters were in bed, Irena sat with Janina at her side and told her parents all that had happened to her since the day the bombs first fell on Radom in 1939. She relived those fearful days of near starvation in the forest and then she whispered the horrible truth of the brutal rape. Amid tears of painful memories, Irena's father tenderly counseled his beloved daughter, telling her that war makes beasts of some men. However, she must not allow these heinous crimes against her to ruin her life. No doubt she could have died, but God did not let that happen. He told Irena that God had preserved her life for a great purpose.

This testimony of a righteous father to his eldest daughter was unquestionably true and prophetic. The Talmud declares: "Whoever destroys one life is as if he destroyed a whole world, and whoever preserves one life is as if he preserved a whole world." There is no hyperbole in this statement. Look at the nations which look to Abraham as the progenitor of their world. His descendants are numberless—millions upon millions. What if the King of Gerar had slain Abraham before he had begotten his sons Issac and Ishmael? In that one act of murder worlds would have been destroyed! The King, however, spared Abraham and restored his wife unto him. Over the course of 4,000 years worlds of his posterity have been born both in Islam and Israel! Each life is designed to beget more life; generations of the yet unborn are dependant upon the now living.

To this point in her life Irena had striven with all of her heart to serve others. She had administered relief to the sick and injured and had done all that she could to save life. Yet when it came to survival, her primary responsibility had been to save herself. To save one's self honorably in times of extreme duress can be the most difficult challenge of life—how much easier it is to give up, to abandon the fight, to die. But Irena did not desert life and in this process of *enduring* she learned how to trust in God and she learned how to be *led* by Him. Thus schooled she could now be instrumental in His hands to save many others. She would shortly be given the opportunity to preserve the lives of innocent Jews who, without her protection, would certainly die. She would soon be presented with choices that would appear contrary to self-preservation. To choose the right would require that she risk her own life daily and do so against impossible odds. "God has plans for you," her father had said and he might have continued, "God wants you to save worlds."

The peace and delectation of Irena's reunion with her family was but the eye of the storm. Out of war's fury had come a moment of calm. In this brief respite she had found healing, profound fatherly guidance and renewed familial love. She was now strengthened for the return of the hurricane.

Without warning the Nazi's tore Wladyslaw from his wife and children. He was compelled to return to Kozlowa Gora to oversee factory equipment that he had formerly designed which the Germans did not have the knowledge to operate. Although his position was vital, it was a condition of slave labor and he was given next to nothing on which to live. After it became apparent that he would not be allowed to return to Radom, Irena's mother took the younger children and joined him. Irena and Janina stayed with their Aunt Helen working wherever they could to eke out a living. Several weeks later as Irena attended church, the sanctuary was suddenly violated by a *lapanka*, a German round up. There was a fearful confrontation between the German soldiers and two priests. The armed soldiers, of course, prevailed. All were ordered out of the church and the physically fit were loaded into trucks. These civilians became conscripts of the *Reich*.

Some of the newly forced laborers were sent to Germany, but Irena was assigned to work in the ammunition factory right in Radom. It was absolute subjugation. She worked standing endlessly ensconced in a toxic atmosphere of gun powder and slept in cold over-crowded barracks. Her lungs tried to expel the noxious dew and she coughed constantly. Day by day she became weaker and fought ever growing vertigo. To complain to the German guards or to faint was to be taken away, never to be heard of again. One day her struggle came to an end. The chief officer who ran the plant, Major Rügemer, was inspecting Irena's department. As he approached her station, she was overpowered by the fumes and lost consciousness.

When she awakened she was surprised to find herself resting comfortably in the Major's office. He asked her for her name and she responded, "*Irene* Gut." Even in her weakened condition he was obviously attracted by her Nordic good looks. Her name sounded Germanic but she admitted she was Polish. He was impressed by her command of his language and her frank honest manner. She begged him not to send her away, pleading that she had a younger sister in Radom—and that she was normally strong and fit for hard work. He was silent for what seemed an eternity. Her fate was totally in his hands. Finally he spoke. He told her that she was wasted on the assembly line and that her ability to speak both

German and Polish could be very useful to Herr Schultz who ran the officer's kitchen. She would be allowed, he explained, to live at home as long as she reported to work each morning at 7:00 a.m. She couldn't believe her good fortune! She was literally starving and in the ammunition factory she was being poisoned by chemicals. Now instead of filling bullets she would be preparing aromatic food fit for the commanding officers. When she arrived home that evening her Aunt Helen and her sister, Janina, could scarcely believe they were once again reunited.

Herr Schultz was a good man who immediately took a fatherly liking to Irene. He was rotund and of a happy disposition. He fed her generously and even allowed her to take food home to her sister and Aunt. Weeks passed quickly and although they had not heard from their parents, Irene and Janina felt very blessed. They had each other and their Aunt. Winter was approaching, they had a comfortable, warm home—and because of the kindness of Herr Shultz, they had plenty to eat. Irene knew that many were not nearly so fortunate, especially the Jews who were forced to live in the ghetto. But she had no idea of how desperate the plight of the Jews had become.

The Officers Mess was an elegant old four-story hotel. Irene had only worked downstairs where there were no windows that faced the back of the building. Behind the hotel was a high wooden fence topped with barbed wire. Beyond the fence was the Glinice Ghetto, the prison of the Jews. One day Shultz asked Irene to set the tables in the fourth floor ballroom which was located at the rear of the hotel. This room had windows that afforded an excellent view into the sad and blighted world of the banished race. Irene parted the velvet drapes and gazed upon the melancholy sight.

The ghetto at first glance looked abandoned, dark and empty. But as she looked, she began to gradually see that there were people here and there in the shadows; one woman crossing the vacant street, a couple of children moving carefully through the snow, and old man standing near a shop door. Cautiously, Jews moved in the dismal streets. Irene felt somehow guilty for being well-fed and safe.

As she went back to work, Irene mused upon the scene of quiet fear. Then suddenly the silent winter afternoon was rent by the sharp sounds of gunfire! She raced back to the window. The dark streets had erupted "like an anthill kicked to pieces." There, before her very eyes, Jews were running for their lives. Children, men, women, young, and old—all fleeing from the horror of deadly SS men leaping from their trucks and openly firing upon the crowds. Bodies fell, police dogs attacked those who tried to run, the snowy streets were covered with blood. Irene stood stunned, unable to move or breathe. As the bullets flew, she felt that she herself was being pierced. She opened her lips to scream, but suddenly a hand pressed over her mouth. It was Shultz. Irene began to struggle, but he held her firmly and his own face was shocked, white, and covered with perspiration. Commanding her to be still, he pulled her from the window, the heavy drapes closed over the agonizing scene. Shultz made Irene look up at him. Then again and again he told her she had not seen this; she must never ever speak of it or even cry. For they would think she was a "Jew-lover" and terrible things happened to "Jew-lovers." He said she could go home and he would cover for her, reporting that she had become ill. "But," he said to her, "you must come back tomorrow at the usual time. And you must tell yourself you never saw this. Now go."

What can one person do? Certainly an army can fight an army. But what could Irene do—a young girl, only nineteen years of age, against the storm troopers of Hell? Most people would have tried to follow the sane advice of Shultz. He was a German, but he was not a Nazi—he was a good man who also had to leave his family behind and was compelled to serve the military. He hated the atrocities but he had resigned himself that there was nothing he could do to prevent the death and misery beyond the fence; and if he could not ameliorate the plight of the poor Jews then certainly he felt that little Irene could do nothing. By now he was very fond of this vivacious blue-eyed Pole. For her own well being he said that she must forget the truth that she now knew.

Irene was not "most people." We would say that Irene was faced with two choices: should she risk self or save self? According to the Nazi overlords it was a capital crime to help a Jew in any way. We would reason that not only her life was dependent upon the choice of self-preservation but also the lives of her sister, her Aunt and her Aunt's children. She did not personally know these Jewish people—should she not look to saving herself and her own kin? But for this Polish Heroine there was only one choice open to her.

"I did not ask myself, Should I do this? But how will I do this? Every step of my childhood had brought me to this crossroad; I must take the right path, or I would no longer be myself."

The following day Irene took what appeared to be a pail of garbage out into the back alley. She looked around and could see no one. She removed from her apron a large metal spoon and knelt at the base of the horrible wooden fence. Soon she had dug a small hole beneath the fence the size of a loaf of bread. She pushed aside potato peelings in the garbage pail and withdrew a tin box filled with fresh food and slid the tin beneath the fence—then dashed back into the kitchen. The next day she found the tin in the hole—empty. Irene asked Shultz if her sister Janina could work in the kitchen, telling him proudly of her culinary skills. He readily agreed. Every day the two sisters smuggled the life saving food into the ghetto—Janina would stand watch while Irene placed the tin box full of apples and cheese under the fence and later retrieved the empty container. They never saw the beneficiaries of their courage. Did any German know of their conspiracy of mercy? Probably Shultz did—finally he too could do something—he could keep silent.

Months passed and the Germans advanced their eastern front towards Russia. Major Rügemer's ammunition factory was moved to Ternopol, of all places—now held by the Germans. Shultz and his kitchen staff, including Irene and Janina were moved to the new headquarters. The new facility, which also was a converted hotel, was much larger and served enlisted men, many officers and their secretaries. Irene's responsibilities were expanded to include the laundry and the cleaning of the officer's suites and the secretaries' quarters. In Ternopol the ammunition factory and the laundry used Jewish slave labor imported daily from the *Arbeitslager*, or the work camp. Like Radom, Ternopol also had its own heavily guarded Jewish Ghetto. It was a place where exiled Jews were banished until they were rounded up and sent to the ultimate horror of the death camp. Not that the ghetto was free from murder. The elite emissaries of Apollyon, the SS, killed indiscriminately wherever their shadows fell. Only the ghettos did not see the wholesale murder that was the daily occupation of the death camps.

In Ternopol the battalion commander of the SS, the Sturmbannfuhrer, was a young man, about thirty years of age, named Rokita. He possessed the face, features and build of a Norse god with blonde hair and deep blue eyes. But those eyes were frightening—deep blue orbs of death. He wore the black uniform of Hell with the Swastika upon his sleeve and the skull ring upon his finger. Under Rokita, the SS were continually searching for Jews who were still at large, hiding. When found, they were incarcerated in the ghetto. The ghetto was the *Africa* of Jewish Slavery—the hunting grounds of the SS where they would round up the ablest men and women to labor in the work camps. Because the Jewish workers for the *Reich* had a brief life expectancy and as the expanding war required increasing numbers of slaves for the Empire's war machine, the *lapankas* in the ghetto were frequent. The eventual destiny of the ghetto, according to *official* policy was its obliteration—literally. Each town and city was to become *Judenfrei, free from Jews*. The Nazis did not just seek dominion over Judah, they sought to completely exterminate the race. When their "success" had been realized in a city—when every Jewish man, woman and child had been murdered and its ghetto bulldozed into oblivion, the Nazis would post sadistic triumphal signs everywhere which read: *This Town is Jew Free.* Rokita's SS zealously accomplished their *lapankas* in the ghetto, therefore, not just to supply the work camps, but also to fill their quotas for the death trains.

Sense and reason are found only in Heaven. Hell is *non*sense. Even when organized, dark forces conjure conflicting strategies. Ultimately the end of all sinister schemes is chaos. On the one hand, Major Rügemer was required to deliver an enormous supply of ammunition to the German soldiers battling the Russians on the Eastern Front. The bullets were made in his factory manned by Jews. On the other hand, Rokita systematically was responsible for the extermination of the Jews, including the labor force of Rügemer's munitions plant. The inane policies of the *Reich*, however, are far more vacuous when examined under the light of morality.

Irene marveled at the differences between her enemies. The Russian soldiers had been crude, raw and cruel—killing without hesitation. Yet, the Nazis were meticulous and courteous, but devoid of feeling. She called them, "murderers in white gloves." Killers, like Hitler, Stalin and other ruthless leaders, she reasoned, had been able to obtain power because the sleeping populace had not heeded clear warnings. Hitler's book, *Mein Kampf,* had been widely read in Europe and America, but was not taken seriously by the masses. Over 80% of Germany had voted against Hitler, yet he still rose to power and was bent, through brute war, on enslavement and annihilation. Irene, her family, and her polish countryman were literal slaves to Hitler. She marveled at the incomprehensibility of war, of marking the entire Jewish race for extermination. It was apparent to Irene that this was "not just war between members of the human race" but that "the devil himself had engineered this debacle, and was in control of our sad world."

Irene looked and sounded German to the Jewish workers in the laundry and at first they did not trust her. But she made it clear to them from the very beginning that she was Polish and would do all she could to help them. Like the rest of the Jewish workers, they were malnourished. She smuggled food into the laundry hidden in large wash hampers. They had no warm clothing. With the help of Shultz she brought them blankets from which they sewed winter coats. Never knowing when or where a *lapankas* might occur she helped them build a fake shelved wall in the laundry with a hiding place behind it. Over time they not only trusted her, but looked to her as their protector. She was at this time twenty years old. They confided in her their sufferings back in the *Arbeitslager*—and insisted that they, because of Irene, had it better than any of their fellow-Jews. If only she could expand the help she was able to give!

While she secretly gave continual aid to her Jewish friends she was the epitome of organization and management in her assigned duties. Major Rügemer was extremely impressed with Irene's skills in the kitchen, keeping the quarters, and supervising the laundry, which included mending and tailoring. She explained that her success was due to her "good help," referring to the Jews. She mustered the courage to tell him that it was becoming increasingly difficult to maintain her high standards with the growing demands on her staff. She had to have *more helpers*—which meant *more Jews*. The Major looked at Shutlz who readily agreed that Irene had too much to do without more workers. Rügemer smiled at Irene and gave her permission to increase her staff immediately by ten.

Within a couple of days a truck pulled up to the hotel, delivering a young married couple and eight girls. Not knowing what would happen next, they literally trembled with fear. The sight of those poor creatures made Irene want to cry herself—for as yet she didn't even have a plan how to really help them, except to temporarily give them a safe place to work and food to eat. On her young shoulders, in addition to her work responsibilities, the food she was smuggling into the ghetto, and caring for her other Jewish workers—now there were ten more people she must comfort and save from starvation.

Major Rügemer and the *hotel* grew ever more reliant upon Irene. The Major treated her well and Shultz treated her as an equal. Even Rokita liked Irene, although she gave him no occasion to become familiar with her. Rokita spoke freely of the extermination of the Jews and abolishing the Poles, but boasted that they would make good Germans of the "northern types," the "blue-eyed blondes, like Irene!"

Irene had kept her sister hidden, working in the kitchen, whenever Rokita dined. But one day the inevitable happened and Rokita espied the beautiful and tender Janina. Irene was horrified. Immediately she spoke with Major Rügemer and frankly told him her fears for Janina's well being, considering Rokita's obvious intentions. The Major, despite his faults, was cut from an entirely different cloth than the SS Chief. He agreed with Irene and promptly transferred Janina back to Radom. When Rokita learned that Janina was gone he cornered Irene in the kitchen, tightly gripping her arm, demanding to know where Janina was. Irene looked into those ice-cold eyes and lied. She told him that Janina had contracted the highly contagious and deadly disease of tuberculosis. Fearing others might catch it the Major had Janina sent away. Instantly Rokita dropped Irene's arm and grew pale. It was hard for her not to laugh at the frightened look in his eyes. So, she thought, the great Rokita could also be afraid!

As time passed Rokita increased the *lapankas*, thinning out the Jewish population. Irene could see the mounting terror in the faces of her friends in the laundry. Although she was younger than they—she now regarded them as if they were her children. Some wanted to attempt an escape, but there was little chance of that. How could they get out of a town that was the military headquarters of the Reich's eastern offensive with soldiers everywhere? There was ten kilometers of open land before the protective cover of the forest could be reached. How could they travel so far without being seen? Irene told them to wait just a little while and she would find a way to help them. Several days later Irene asked Shultz for permission to visit a friend in the country. He not only granted her leave, but gave her cookies and chocolates to give to her "friends." She left Ternopol driving a horse drawn wagon she had borrowed from a trusted friend. In the back was a small load of hay and a good size sack of potatoes. Beneath the hay was stowed a precious cargo, and for Irene a dangerous one—the Morris brothers and their wives. When the road narrowed beneath the shade of the towering pines Irene stopped the wagon. She cried as she left them in their wilderness haven—she knew how difficult it was to survive in the forest! A week later she made the same journey with Abram Klinger and David Rosen hidden under the straw. Her friends joined with others who had successfully escaped into the woodlands. Their homes were dugouts,

Main Entrance Villa von Trapp

Villa von Trapp

Himmler's Former Office - Villa von Trapp

Susan Hancock with Father Andrea Hasenburger - Villa von Trapp

Author with Father Hasenburger - Balcony off Baron von Trapp's Study

Author's sister (Susan Hancock) with Author - Nonnberg Abby

Caroline Schnöll, in the Garden of Dokterwirt Hotel,
dressed in traditional dirndl similar to what Maria would have worn

Himmler's Wall—built with slave labor around Villa von Trapp

Park next to Villa von Trapp

Aigen Schloss and Chapel where Maria and children practiced and performed

Looking east from Hohensalzburg towards Aigen

Maria's Alps near Zeller See

Alpine Waterfall near her Father's Tragedy

The Execution of Lady Jane Grey by Paul Delaroche. The National Gallery of London

The Offer of the Crown to Lady Jane Grey - In the Gallery of His Grace The Duke of Bedford
C. R. Leslie, R. A. Pinx & Sculp - London

Roger Ascham and Lady Jane Grey
by Henri Joseph Fradelle, Engraved by William Say, 1825
National Portrait Gallery, London

Lady Jane Grey by G. Staal, H. Robinson - New York, D. Appleton & Co.

Arrest of Lady Jane Grey
Engraved by J. Sartain, the original by A. Deveria

The Author with Irene Gut Updyke

Irene in her Garden

Susanna and the Elders
by Jacopo da Empoli
Art History Museum, Vienna

Interrogation of Joan of Arc by Paul Delaroche
Musée des Beaux Arts de Rouen

Village of Domremy, France - Joan of Arc's Village

La Meuse River near Joan's Home

Home of Joan d'Arc with the Chapel of Domremy in the Background

Interior of Chapel Domremy

Hearth in Joan of Arc's Home

Chapel of Notre Dame de Bermont

*Ruins of Vaucouleurs - Photograph taken by Author in February,
the same month as Joan's departure from Vaucouleurs for Chinon*

Ruins of Vaucouleurs

covered with pine boughs. Food was extremely hard to come by. Irene continued to risk her life for these refugees—taking them food, medicines, and whatever supplies she could steal from the Nazis. She accomplished all this while continuing to provide for the remaining six who worked in her laundry.

Often Irene overheard officers discussing critical information while they ate. She was a familiar sight to them and knew how to blend into the background. One hot summer night, while they dined, Irene observed Major Rügemer and Rokita involved in an intense conversation. There was irritation, if not anger, written all over the major's face. She worked her way towards their table, feigning some task. She heard Rügemer exclaim, "What am I supposed to do now? How do I find more workers?" Rokita responded with great calm that his purpose was to warn him in advance, so that he would have time to conscript and train replacements for his Jewish workers. Irene was stunned. She knew this had happened elsewhere, but why here where the slaves of Judah were so needed in Rügemer's munitions plant to fight the Russians? The tray she was carrying crashed to the floor. She excused herself complaining that she had twisted her ankle—but her mind was swimming—Rokita's cold stare pierced her heart as with double daggers. So Ternopol was to be made *Judenfrei*, she thought. All the Jews, including her dear friends, were to be *liquidated*!

That evening Irene knelt by her beside, praying, crying, pleading to God in desperation. In dismay she cried out, "Oh, God, where are you?" Then she felt ashamed of herself for questioning HIM. The night passed with Irene on her knees, her eyes filled with tears. At last she succumbed to sleep. She awoke, still in the obeisant posture, aching and stiff. As the day dawned, frigid and steel gray, the full impact of what she had heard broke upon her sober young mind and she knew what she had to do.

Irene could not conceal the awful news from her friends in the laundry. A young man named Lazar, put his arms around his young wife Ida, as if to protect her from what they had just learned. He looked desperately at Irene, imploring her to help them. She told her dear friends that she did not know what she could do. There might still be a chance, she said, to get them to the forest. She was determined to not let them die!

A week later Major Rügemer summoned Irene to his office and explained that the hotel was becoming quite crowded with new officers and that he had decided to move into a house. He would still do most of his work in his office at the plant, but he would entertain officers at the house instead of the hotel. He wanted her to limit her time at the kitchen and laundry, keep his house and oversee his social functions in his new residence. A thought leaped into Irene's mind. That afternoon she excitedly excused herself with Shultz for several hours and checked out Rügemer's soon to be home. It was a fenced off estate in a quiet part of town surrounded by large trees. The house was two-stories above ground with servant's quarters in a below-ground-cellar. A perfect hiding place; imagine sequestering Jews in a German Major's house!

She couldn't wait to share her plan with her friends in the laundry. Lazar knew the home and said that it was designed by a Jewish architect and was even rumored to have a secret hiding place in it. No doubt this plan was extremely risky but it presented by far the best possible solution available to them. Clara, a young Jewess, exclaimed that this was the hope that they had been praying for. They had faith in God and confidence in Irene!

There was more that Irene felt compelled to do—she could warn the worker Jews in the factory. She borrowed a bicycle and during lunch rode around the perimeter of the complex. Whenever she saw the Star of David on a jacket she would put herself into a position where she could whisper a warning without being noticed. She had become skilled at non-distraction. Softly, without displaying emotion, she would tell them to escape—to hide—that Ternopol was to be *Judenfrei*.

One serious obstacle arose that threatened her plan to hide her friends in Rügemer's basement. The home was currently occupied by illegal occupants, war-squatters. The Major had arranged for them to move into an apartment complex on July 22nd. Then she overheard Rokita tell Rügemer that the 22nd of July was the very day that he would sweep through Ternopol, the complex, the hotel and in one grand *lapankas* send all the Jews to the death camps! Irene was beside herself! She couldn't move her friends into the Major's home until the squatters had moved out. Oh God, she prayed—all she needed was one day, one day!

The fateful day approached and she told her six friends to hide behind the false wall in the laundry on the evening of the 21st—and not to depart with the others back to the work camp. The fake wall could only withstand a cursory inspection and she and they both knew it. It would never fool the trained eyes of the Gestapo! But they did as she directed. All of their hearts stopped beating when the soldiers came later that night—the head count was down in the transport trucks and they had been ordered to scrutinize the entire complex. Irene's legs were like rubber when the Germans entered the laundry; but to them everything looked in order. They all knew it was a narrow escape. What would they do when Rokita's elite conducted the search?

By 6 p.m. the office staff left and Irene went about her usual duties of straightening the Major's suite. She knew it was too dangerous to let her friends remain in the laundry closet. Nor could she take them to Rügemer's new home until the squatters had moved. As she worked, she prayed, "Oh God, what will I do now?" Trembling with fear, she tried to force herself to think of an answer, but there seemed to be no solution.

As she went into the bathroom, she gazed about. Suddenly, her eyes fell upon a square screen, a vent in the ceiling. Irene grabbed a chair and climbing up, was able to remove the cover. There was an air vent at least two meters in length. Could it possibly be large enough and strong enough to bear six people? She felt this was her answer and her only hope. Imagine hiding Jews in the Major's bathroom!

The majority of the officers and secretaries had left their rooms to socialize at the theatre, but there were still enlisted men in residence and two officers with colds who remained in their quarters. Irene took them hot tea and medication to "help them sleep." At 9:30 Irene crept quietly into the laundry room. First she led two, then one at a time from the laundry, down the hallway, and up the three flights of stairs to Rügemer's bathroom. By midnight they were all packed like sardines, hidden in the vent. At 2:00 a.m. the officers began to return from the theatre and with them Major Rügemer. He went to his bed whispering under his breath, "Stupid! Stupid war!" As he slept fitfully six silent guests heard the moans of this troubled aging commander—only a few feet away!

The next day was equally dramatic. Irene had opened an entrance into the hiding place in the laundry and had placed buckets and mops there— giving it the appearance of an odd storage closet. Not long thereafter the Gestapo arrived and swarmed over the place "like ants on a hill." Irene avoided them and went up to check on her fugitives. As she entered the major's suite and turned towards the bathroom her heart stopped completely—she came face to face with an SS officer! He had been using the major's facilities. Excusing himself, he laughed and swaggered past her. Irene was not the only one terrified by the close call. Hoping to see Irene, when the bathroom door opened, the cramped Jews were horrified at seeing an SS officer standing below them! When Irene arrived, they urged her to put an end to their misery, turn them in and save herself at least. Irene was firm as she responded that her life was not worth more than theirs. She told them to be still—they would not give up, they had already come too far. She promised them they would be safe that very night. However, she sounded more self-assured than she felt.

The day dragged on mercilessly slow while the Gestapo performed with exactness this final round up. They found enough victims to satisfy their bloodlust, for the awful silence that prevailed was frequently shattered by the repercussions of gunfire. Everyone knew that each shock wave was an execution.

The major did not go out that night but retired at ten o'clock! What were they to do? Again Irene prayed fervently. As he bid Shultz and Irene good night he muttered that he was exhausted, probably from his short fitful sleep of the night before and the strain of the appalling events of that endless day. He asked Irene to bring him some hot milk and mumbled that he was going to take something to help him sleep. His confession was music to her ears! She waited a while, then cautiously entered his room. If he awoke, all was lost! She went to his bedside and from the nightstand stole his keys—she would need them to unlock the backdoor of the hotel. She led her frightened comrades, two at a time, past the sleeping major, down the three flights of stairs, past the dining room, down the silent streets to their "safe house," then helped them down the coal chute into the cellar. At two in the morning her incredible feat was completed and she quietly returned the key ring to the major's quarters. Then ghostlike, she crept to her own room and finally rested.

Besides the original six from the laundry, four others joined Irene's *family* hidden in the cellar. One was the Jewish husband of her dear friend Helen. The others were men she did not know, but sheltered nonetheless. Shultz provided Irene with enough food to supply her guests and food for her continued trips to the forest, never asking questions, and always reassuring her that she could have whatever *she needed*. On one of these sylvan trips she found Herman Morris terribly distraught. His wife Meriam was feverish, her lungs weak with possible pneumonia. He cried to Irene, "She will die and I will die with her." She knew it was true if

Meriam remained in that awful dugout. Now Irene smuggled Jews into Ternopol! Meriam and Herman Morris joined her subterranean guests bringing the total to an even dozen.

The rumor that Lazar had heard regarding the secret hiding place in the major's house proved to be true! Ingeniously hidden behind a removable coal chute was a tunnel that led underground to a room fashioned below a gazebo. There were air vents that were built into the stone façade that were nearly invisible when looking at the gazebo from the outside. Soon their bunker was stocked with food and water. Rügemer's movements were predictable and he never ventured into the cellar but whenever he entertained, the twelve Jews hid safely underground beneath the shaded structure. The challenges, however, were continual. Clara approached Irene one day with the news that Ida was pregnant and matter-of-factly asked her to help her end the pregnancy. What else could they do, she argued for the group, a baby's cry would doom them all!

Irene answered emphatically, "No!" They should not even consider abortion as an option. Hitler had killed too many children already and they must not let him destroy this child as well. As they had pled for their own lives, Irene pled for the life of this unborn baby. "Please, let it live!" She promised that everything would turn out fine and even foretold that they would be free before the baby's birth. Although Irene was very young, she was not naïve. She had already experienced a lifetime of sorrows; yet, because of her incredible faith, had witnessed many times the miraculous intervening hand of God. She believed this pregnancy was a sign from Him—that He was bringing "new life from the ashes of those who had died in the flames."

Her words were prophetic. Before Ida gave birth, the Russians pushed the Germans back from Ternopol. Irene was warned by Major Rügemer just before they pulled back. With her borrowed horse and wagon, Irene once again made the perilous trips to the forest, smuggling her dear friends from the cellar to the haven in the wilderness—all but Ida and one other of her stowaways, Fanka. She hid these two women with a forester named Sigmund Pashefski. Irene had made friends of Sigmund and his wife during her many trips into the country and had wisely taken them into her confidence. She had discovered that Pashefski was with the *Resistance* and he gladly provided the shelter needed to bring Ida's child safely into the world.

Sigmund proved to be extremely important to Irene in another way. In the sudden German retreat and evacuation of Ternopol, Irene had lost her purpose—suddenly she was no longer responsible for the lives of her twelve dear companions. No longer could she help sustain the lives of her friends in the forest. For the first time since she stopped being *Rachel* and started being *Irene* she was responsible only for herself! It had been such a long time and her *mission* had been of life and death importance. Through her superhuman effort and by the blessing of Heaven she had been entirely successful. But now she was released from it all, and the relief was not as welcome as she had perhaps imagined it would be. That is the way it is when we have been *needed* desperately and find ourselves displaced from the former necessity. The loss she felt in her soul was akin to what a mother feels when her children are finally reared and leave the shadow of her protective wing. This type of emptiness can only be filled by a new and noble purpose. Almost without her realizing it her thoughts ascended to heaven in the form of a question: What would You *now* have me do? It was Sigmund who opened the doorway into her next *existence*.

Just as Major Rügemer had taken Irene with him when he moved his headquarters to Ternopol, now he planned to have her accompany him to Kielce. Kielce was to be the new control center where the Germans hoped to launch their counteroffensive against the Russians. When Sigmund learned that Kielce was Irene's destination he gave her his brother-in-law's address and a code name: *Mercedes-Benz*. He explained that the partisans were well organized there, and she must slip away from the Germans in Kielce to join the resistance. He hugged and kissed her saying that she was a "true soldier."

It was a tiring journey to Kielce. Rügemer had long been used to granting Irene autonomy and she had never even attempted flight. Of course it had been under his protective umbrella that she had been able to accomplish so great an undertaking. All that had changed overnight but the major had not understood the substance of her loyalty. Upon their arrival he simply checked her into a hotel and told her he would call for her when he was settled in his new assignment. No escape was necessary. She simply went to bed and the following day walked out of the hotel, and in that simple act of leaving resigned her service to the *Third Reich*. She never saw Major Rügemer again.

As she walked through the streets of Kielce she again used her skill of merging into her surroundings. She had come a long way since her foolish outing in the park of Ternopol waiting for her train. She knew now what it meant to be stopped without papers and carefully found her way to the memorized address Sigmund had given her. A lovely, middle-aged woman answered the door suspiciously. However, when Irene said that she had been sent by the forester Pashefski to speak of *Mercedes-Benz*, immediately the woman's countenance changed. She cordially invited Irene to stay for lunch and as she worked in the kitchen, she inquired about Sigmund Pashefski, her brother. Then her husband entered, a tall man with gray hair and vivid blue eyes. When he heard of Irene's work to save others, the kindly man invited her to stay with their family, saying how privileged they were to know her.

When again the door swung open a strikingly handsome young man entered the room. He was introduced as their son, Janek. Irene looked up into his eyes as he shook her hand. His face was expressive, his hair lustrous and dark, his handgrip strong, yet warm and friendly. Immediately Irene felt herself charmed and enchanted under his gaze. There was a moment when neither of these young people spoke. It was Janek who broke the silence, "I understand you're looking for me. *Mercedes Benz* is my code name. I'm a leader with the local partisans."

You may say what you wish about love at first sight—about the foolishness of the young and immature. But Irene, although still extremely young, was anything but juvenile. True love is the recognition of virtue. As Irene looked into his eyes she saw the antithesis of Rokita. In an instant she saw *light* and the passion of liberty in Janek's courageous gaze. He might have thought himself ordinary. But Irene, who had been refined in the unspeakable fires of adversity, whose judgement of human nature was now proven beyond question, saw and felt in this young freedom-fighter all of the manly virtues of true integrity—and she straightway loved him for it. And Janek saw in this beautiful golden-haired heroine a vision which all of her former tormentors were incapable of seeing. He saw her loveliness and *sensed* her divine nature. It was the meeting and the attraction of two great souls.

Years had passed since Irena had left Kovno with that small remnant of the defeated Polish Army. The *Resistance* had become organized, skilled, and had connections with the rightful Polish government in exile in England. The partisans welcomed the brave Irene into their covert militia and gave her the code name *Mala*! Again she routinely risked her life and in the manner to which she had become expert. She was not asked to wield a gun and join in the frequent raids against their enemies. Such action, at least, had the benefit of companionship in battle. No, she was once again to demonstrate solitary fortitude.

Her particular assignment was to deliver and receive communications from spies who passed information about German objectives on to Mala. Her missions were critical and perilous. She dressed as a "common *hausfrau*," and in her hair, done carefully in a bun, she hid secret messages.

Mala traveled inconspicuously by bicycle and always with a capsule of poison to quickly take her own life should she ever be arrested. This was the only way a partisan could be sure of not betraying compatriots if captured—for torture and coerced confession would surely follow. Her quick wit and cool head gave her extraordinary success. For example, one day as Mala was on assignment, she emerged from the forest. Immediately, she was stopped by a German patrol. They questioned where she was coming from. Mala had been in so many dangerous encounters previously, she had no difficulty coming up with a plausible lie. She answered that she had suddenly experienced an "intestinal crisis" and had dashed into the woods for relief. The Germans laughed heartily and allowed Mala to pass without even asking for identification. On another occasion, Mala carried a parcel in a basket on her bike's handlebars. Thousands of British pounds were wrapped inside the parcel—valuable contraband to finance the Polish underground. As she rode across a guarded bridge she was stopped by an officer. Mala smiled at the young man, using her best German and twisted her golden curls as she flirted with him. She knew full well he would be looking at her rather than at the valuable parcel. She promised the guard that she would return after visiting her mother. Once again she passed unhindered.

It was a season not only of daring, but of wonderful courtship. Mala said "yes" to her handsome freedom fighter and their wedding date was set for May 5th, her birthday. On the 2nd of May her mother-in-law-to-be was hemming Mala's bridal gown when her groom burst into the room and, discarding the old wive's tale of seeing his betrothed in her wedding dress before the wedding, swept her into his arms and kissed her passionately. He had come to speak with her with some urgency; but seeing her in such a manner he had totally forgotten the purpose of his coming. When the kiss ended, he laughed and chided her for causing a lapse of memory and struggled to recall his errand. Then he said, "We just got word—a German transport is moving through the forest tonight. We're going to hit it. We need the ammunition." Seeing her countenance immediately fall, he reassured her that it would be an easy target and she must not worry. Then he was gone.

As night fell she was struck with an awful premonition. Her heart began to race and she could not silence the voice of terrible dread that cried mightily within her. Later in the evening a sobbing mother held Mala in her arms, weeping uncontrollably. The underground had taken the German transport successfully, but not without casualties. Mercedes was dead.

Mala was overwhelmed with sorrow—simply stunned. Over and over again she asked the question: Why? Why was she struck with such a tragedy just as she was finally beginning to live? All of the joyful dreams that she and Janik had lovingly built suddenly vanished. Now, Mala was alone and felt nothing was left. The bleak emptiness of life was suffocating; she longed to be free of pain by fading into numbing death.

Mala took her grief to a friend and counselor, a wise old priest, Father Joseph. He was a devout servant of the Lord and though she spent hours trying to place the blame of this awful tragedy upon God, he simply would not let her give up her faith. He told her:

> "Satan tempts us in order to bring out the worst in us, and God tests us to bring out the best in us. Your job here isn't finished yet. The Lord gives us different assignments in life. Look at the miracles He has performed in your own life. Don't demand too much. Repent and ask Him for forgiveness, and His love and mercy will heal your pain. That's a promise!"

Mala knew that Father Joseph was right. As she looked into his unfaltering, loving eyes, her frigid heart began to thaw. She felt renewed—her faith in God and her faith in her life's mission restored.

Mala continued her work with the Resistance until the war ended—but the end of World War II did not mean freedom for Poland. The Allies were beguiled into handing over this sad war-torn nation to the Soviet Union! By now the story of Irena, who became Iruska, who became

Rachel, who became Irene, who became Mala the freedom fighter was known, if not to the outside world—was known to the Soviet Secret Police. In fact the Russians believed that she was the chief of the partisans! She was completely unaware of her importance in the eyes of the Soviets.

Ida and Lazar Haller, she discovered, were now living in Katowice. How she longed to see Ida and her miracle child Roman—the baby she had saved. Little did she know that she was about to be captured by the Russians for the *third* time! How did this happen? Although government officials publicly announced that partisans who voluntarily declared themselves members of the underground would be granted amnesty, Mala was not duped by this ploy and stayed incognito. She felt safe—after all, she had evaded authorities for such a long time. Nonetheless she relaxed her guard. As she made her way to Ida's home, and just two blocks from her apartment, she was recognized by the police, arrested and incarcerated. Predictably, she was then interrogated and terrorized.

Hour after hour, day after day, they demanded the names and ranks of resistance fighters. They wanted to know every detail of the underground organization. Mala renounced knowledge of everything. She was placed in a locked room where, exhausted, she was allowed to fall asleep. But the moment she did so, she was awakened and interrogated over and over again. Even though Mala denied all they accused her of, she felt certain the inquisitors could see through her lies. As she was apprehended secretly there was no one who could come to her aid. Her only help and her only hope was God. To Him, night and day, her prayers for delivery continually ascended.

She was forced to work during daylight hours, scrubbing and cleaning. Then, extremely fatigued, she would collapse into deep sleep. But her tormentors would not allow her to rest, but would awaken her "every hour, on the hour" and resume their relentless questioning. Acutely deprived of sleep, Mala lost track of time, as everything in her life became a confusing blur.

One day she was working in the upstairs hallway when she felt a cold breeze from an open window. She turned and looked at the window and noticed that its iron bars had been placed wider apart than usual. Could she fit through them? Was this the answer to her prayers? Carefully she slid her slender body between the bars and leaped from the second story to the hard ground below. This daring act was not without injury, and initially, she could not walk, but crawled on her hands and knees into the cover of a garden. Several veins in her feet had burst on impact, but no bones appeared broken. She caught her breath and somehow gained the strength to walk upon feet that were "swollen like two balloons"—and made her way to the Haller's apartment. When they saw her on their doorstop they could not believe their eyes. It was not that she surprised them by showing up unexpectedly—they were surprised because she was alive! Their Rabbi had told them that Irene had been arrested—what hope was there that she would survive! There was no time now for a reunion— it was time for flight! Ida's brother caught her reeling in his arms and carried her off the porch and quickly hid her in their wash room! Irena thought of the irony of it all. Her laundry in Ternopol had been a place of refuge for Ida and her Husband Lazar, and now they were hiding her from her enemies in their laundry.

The next thing she knew the Hallers had bundled her in a car and she was on her way to Krakow. There another of the Jews she had saved gave her sanctuary until her feet healed. During her convalescence she received heartrending news from Ida who had sought diligently to uncover information regarding the welfare of her family. The Germans murdered her father in 1945. The Russian secret police were combing the country for her, and worst of all, they had arrested her mother and four sisters. Three weeks later she received a wonderful report from the Hallers—the Russians were convinced that her family had no idea where Irene was and they were released.

The Jews had their own secret network and soon all of those whom she had hid in Rügemer's cellar came to see her—what a grand and glorious gathering! They wrote her miraculous story and witnessed how she had saved their lives. They notarized their testimonial and gave it to the Jewish Historical Committee in Krakow. Irene, with her friends, knew that her life was in constant jeopardy as long as she remained in Poland— a Poland that was held tight in the *red grip*. Irene's mother and sisters were thought to be under surveillance by the secret police hoping to apprehend *Mala*, still alleged by the Russians to be the leader of the underground. Irene's Jewish friends used their influence to make provisions with a Jewish relocation organization to get her out of the country and into a camp in Bavaria. They dyed Irene's golden hair jet black and gave her a new name: *Sonia Sofierstein*. Her forged papers were flawless and her passage to Germany was marred only by the awful grief she bore in her heart as she left her beloved homeland for what she felt would be forever.

The Jewish relocation camp in Hessich-Lichtenau to which Sonia was sent was a little town 150 kilometers north of Frankfurt. It was a restful place in the country built new by reparation funds from defeated Germany. Her community consisted of approximately 250 Jews of all ages. Each resident had lived through many horrors and in some cases, was the only surviving member of their family. The surrealism of their new life seemed like a dream in contradistinction to their recent past— entirely incongruous with reason. At first the habitual distrust and innate fear born of the unspeakable atrocities they had survived created a heavy atmosphere of dreadful isolation. Sonia was overwhelmed with self-sorrow and longed for someone who would be her *friend*. But never did she loose her sense of gratitude to God and His creative Hand.

Sonia listened to the quiet voice of the Spirit that penetrated her mind and heart. She acted as her own psychiatrist by continually reminding herself that her life had been spared for a reason. God had blessed her with capable hands, an intellect and talents which He expected her to use to help others—and now she was blessed with freedom! Sonia would use that freedom to spread love, friendship, and after all of the deprivation that her fellow survivors had endured, she would spread tolerance. Then, when despair threatened her heart—she counted her blessings, squared her shoulders, rolled up her sleeves and went to work serving others.

It was July 1946 and Bavaria was gloriously beautiful. Sonia loved the deep greens of the hills splashed with blossoms. Nature was alive with the songs of birds. Trees were dressed in luxuriant verdure. She felt that: "all seemed to promise hope for the future to mend our broken lives." She returned to her nursing studies and was soon working in the camp dispensary, again blessing the lives of the sick and afflicted. Sonia also studied Hebrew with the Rabbi. She wrote to her friends in Krakow under her new identity to learn of news from home. The help she continually offered others in the Hessich-Lichtenau camp soon made her many friends.

Sonia awakened each day to a new sense of wonder in the grandeur of forest, mountains, and flower fields. She felt in all of this beauty, surely she was healing from the horror of past years. Again, gratitude for life itself filled her soul and she felt her confidence in the future growing as surely as the flora of Bavaria. When disappointments came, Sonia found comfort in the woods. She picked berries for jam to give away. She also shared baked goods and found there was a direct relationship between the healing of her heart and the service that she gave. As the days passed, the other members of the camp joined Sonia in laughter and pleasant conversation.

In spare moments, she began decorating her bare room. From discarded boxes she fashioned furniture, from used colorful blankets she made a bedspread, from medical gauze she created window curtains. Even colored paper was transformed into picture frames and bottles into vases for her bouquets of wildflowers or green boughs. The change was a magnet drawing everyone to the colors, scents, and freshness of Sonia's room.

It was just not Sonia's room her friends came to admire. It was to Sonia herself they came. The cheerful room was but a reflection of a soul incapable of despair. She was a *healer*. Although she knew how to nurture the body, she knew far more how to nourish the soul through absolute faith in God, through gratitude for every blessing regardless how small, through inspired optimism, through service, and through study. She lived three and a half years in this village. Life still brought her challenges—the stuff of which true living is made. She contracted diphtheria, perhaps from her service in the dispensary—but again she recovered. By the time the summer of 1947 was gone her blonde hair had grown out. By then everyone knew her story—how she was not a Jew, but was a savior of Jews. She was loved—how she was loved by these wonderful survivors! *Sonia was now known again as Irena*. The circle of her life was complete. She was still herself.

How many of us can look back, after some great tragedy has tried us thoroughly, and can say that we are still ourselves? How many sorrowful persons readily admit that their compromises have sold them, molded them into something alien from their own soul? *The girl with many names*, was always true to self, true to God and true to her fellowman. That is why she worthy of the title *Heroine*.

In early autumn she was sought out by a United Nations delegate, William K. Opdyke. After hearing her phenomenal history he greatly marveled. He knew that he was in the presence of a woman of uncommon courage and integrity. He invited her, formally, to become a U.S. citizen.

Irena soon made the crossing to America and was thrilled beyond description when she first beheld our Lady of Liberty and was overcome with emotion. She arrived without the benefit of family, without the ability to speak English, and without money. By today's standards she was impoverished. Yet she felt marvelously rich, for she was entering the United States of America—the land of limitless opportunity and freedom! When she first set foot upon American soil she felt like "kneeling down and kissing the earth." Many people today, who categorize themselves as poor, feel that they are entitled to handouts—that for some reason our nation owes them a living. Not so with our young, penniless, Polish heroine who felt indebted beyond measure to America for taking her in. She made a promise that she would live a life worthy of her new country.

Irena adopted the more American sounding name of Irene and pursued each potential opportunity to the fullest. She studied English, worked in a clothing factory, and despite the language barrier became self-reliant! Sometime later she ran across William Opdyke in a coffee shop near the United Nations. He saw her first and immediately recognized her. "I know you!" he said, but she did not make the connection between the distinguished man standing in front of her and the man that had recommended her immigration, nearly two years earlier. "I'm sorry," she responded, I don't believe that I know you." He then began to tell her, her own story with impressive understanding and genuine warmth. She looked at him again. He was tall and handsome, older than she, dark hair with the first signs of gray at his temples. Her mind flashed back to their meeting in Hessich-Lichtenau and she remembered who he was. How different things were now! Now she was independent in a free land with her whole life still before her. He asked her to dinner. She accepted. Each date ended with a supplication from *Bill* for yet another date. Their courting grew into friendship, companionship and deep love.

Bill's life, she discovered, had also been beset with great sadness and nearly insurmountable challenges. His sorrow had schooled him into a discriminator of character. His grief had increased his capacity for *appreciation*—and how he appreciated and cherished Irene. These two survivors, survivors of the greatest conflict the world has yet seen, received true and lasting peace. They found in each other enduring refuge, comfort and happiness. Several months later they were married and moved to beautiful southern California.

Irene started on yet another new beginning. This time, however, her adventures were set on a stage of security and contentment. Bill took her everywhere to see the endless sights of this marvelous God-blessed land. In particular she was moved beyond description when she walked hand in hand with her husband through the forest of the Great Redwoods. Then came the grandest adventure of them all—she gave birth to a beautiful baby daughter. Irene, the lover of life now became a *creator* of life. They named their infant girl Janina, after Irene's beloved sister. Life settled down for the Opdykes and the bitter past became all but forgotten. It was wonderful not to have to even think of the atrocities she had both seen and endured.

However, in the 1970s there arose a ludicrous controversy in our country. Pseudo intellectuals, *history revisionists*, proclaimed that the Jewish Holocaust had been greatly exaggerated. Some proclaimed that the Polish people, not the Nazis, were the ones guilty of war crimes. These liars were given national media attention. Irene was shocked.

"I said to myself, Oh Lord, what should I do? Get angry and forget it? No! I will speak! Help me!"

It was so difficult to open the doors of her girlhood and share with others the nightmare that she had lived through. But she knew that she must do this. A new generation had been born that had no personal experience with the awful consequences of hate. She had witnessed how the deterioration of values paralleled the rise of bigotry—and the end result—a society with no regard for the sanctity of life. She knew that she must do all that was within her power to teach the truth, especially to the youth. She made herself available to school classes, civic groups, church groups. Secular and ecclesiastical leaders recognized her as a gifted teacher with a vital message that must be heard.

In 1982 she finally met Ida's son, Roman Haller, now a grown man. In 1985 she was reunited with her four sisters, Janina, Wladzia, Maria and Bronia who live to this day (December, 1999) and reside in Poland. After fleeing her homeland she never saw her mother again. Mamusia died in 1957, long before Poland was truly liberated from tyranny. She does not know what happened to Dr. David and Dr. Meriam, those two dear friends that had conspired to save her life. The tacitly confederate Shultz, who provided the food that sustained herself and her loved ones, was killed by the Russians during the German retreat from Ternopol. Rokita, the

Gestapo Chief, was arrested and condemned for his countless murders. Ironically, during his trial Rokita wrote to Janina requesting that she testify on his behalf—still thinking that his dashing good looks and charm could sway the young girl that had fled his advances. Janina resolutely refused to aid the devilish war criminal. Major Rügemer was left homeless and penniless after the war. Providentially and ironically, the old man was found wandering by Ida and Clara. Through the Jewish community they secured a room for Rügemer and provided him the necessities of life until his death in the early 1950s.

For the past twenty-five years Irene Gut Opdyke has given selflessly of her time in this last crusade of her life. Irene, now in her 80s, possesses a mind of great celerity. She still speaks frequently to audiences and congregations that cross the boundaries of race, religion and culture. Although her message is one that needs to be heard, regardless of age, Irene feels that it is especially important to teach these truths to the young. What does she tell them? In answer to that question Irene told this author:

"I tell them, I love you. I am here because I love you. And I am here because to me you are the most important people. Learn, study—you can be what you want to be! Don't hurt anyone. If you see someone act in hatred, tell them, 'STOP IT! We all belong to one human family. Stop it!' If you don't do this, then they think they have a right to hate. Then they become Nazis, or Skinheads, or Klu Klux Klan. They are losers! And you, you are not! You are the future leaders of our world."

After she speaks to her young audiences they often line up to shake her hand. She takes their hand in hers and hugs them with pure motherly affection. She said to me,

"So many young people today just need a hug."

Irene lives still in Southern California in a small but beautiful apartment. When I met her, I was immediately struck by her petite frame, her loveliness, and that which is so difficult to describe, her *presence*. She possesses an authority of goodness, a credibility earned through suffering, valiant service and sacrifice. There is about her an aura of great strength and godliness. On Irene's walls hang photographs of her beloved husband, now deceased, pictures of her sisters, her daughter and grandson and photographs of some of those whose lives she saved. These relationships are her treasures. Also on her walls are numerous citations from senates, from cities, from churches, from schools, from distinguished societies and associations. All pay tribute to this small woman who defied the tyranny of Nazi Germany and Soviet Russia and held the sanctity of the lives of others more precious than her own safety. Irene is one of the few *gentiles* ever to be awarded the Israeli Medal of Honor by the Yad Vashem Study Center and Memorial to the Holocaust. In memory of her heroic life-saving service to "worlds" of Jews, an olive tree bears her name on the *Avenue of the Righteous Gentiles* in Israel.

What is in a name? When the name represents a divinely appointed mission the name embodies the sum total of the accomplishments attributed to the one *sent*. *Irena*, the child who became the student nurse, who risked her life to save the victims of the awful Blitzkrieg on Poland, the beautiful winter wanderer in enemy occupied territory, whose innocence was crushed and trampled like a snowflake underfoot, and yet survived virtuous and whole. *Iruska*, the same girl with a new name and a new mission, the nurse who ministered to her enemies soldiers, who grew in medical skill and knowledge, who defied moral assailants and risked her mortal life in a daring escape rather than submit to immoral servitude. *Rachel*, the selfless servant of the peasantry, the accomplished nurse who willingly exposed herself to the dreaded typhoid fever to save life with no thought of compensation, the bold traveler who left the security of a happy and safe existence to traverse the same adversarial regions from which she had fled in the hope only of being reunited with her loved ones, and who in the attempt was captured and incarcerated. *Irene*, the beautiful maiden of pure Arian features, who rose from a munitions factory slave to become the trusted assistant of a major in the German army, a noble heroine who used her enviable position, not to retreat from the horrors of war, but to literally win the lives of men, women and a *baby* from the certainty of Nazi decreed death, at the risk of her own life—not in a singular moment of bravery, but every day of her life for years! *Mala*, signal member of the Polish Resistance, espionage agent, deliverer of crucial communications, smuggler of huge quantities of vital cash to bear the demands of battle, betrothed to the handsome Mercedes, head of the Underground, damsel of grief, widowed before she was married, hunted relentlessly, caught and imprisoned, delivered by Heaven. *Sonia,* adopted by Israel who saved their young savior, light in the yet murky dawn in the camp of survivors, friend to the few who outlived Hitler's genocide, giver of flowers and of hope in the future.

Irena, soul of the woman who retains every name, with their virtues, their honors, the rewards of their divine missions fulfilled, the woman blessed and sanctified by the true love of a noble husband, the heroine recognized world-wide by dignitaries and statesman, and most importantly by the King of Heaven. As this author took leave of the one living heroine of this book, she embraced me, then, with a fixed determination, she took my face into her hands, looked deeply into my eyes and said:

> "This is not my work—this is my mission. God spoke to my heart. I did not hear a voice. I heard in my heart. I am a fighter. I am for the truth. I believe in God."

Bibliography
Primary Sources
Opdyke, Irene Gut & Armstrong, Jennifer: *In My Hands* (Random House Inc., New York)
Opdyke, Irene Gut & Elliot, Jeffrey M: *Into the Flames* (The Borgo Press, San Bernardino)
Personal interview with Irene Gut Opdyke in December of 1999.

The Beauty of Susanna

*For dowry, she had gold and pearls; but the gold was on her head and
the pearls were in her mouth . . . A brilliant face, delicate profile, eyes
of a deep blue, heavy eyelashes, small, arching feet, wrists and ankles
neatly turned . . . a cheek small and fresh, a robust neck . . . the nape
firm and supple, shoulders modeled as if by Coustou, . . . a gaiety
tempered with dreaminess; sculptured and exquisite—[She] was
beautiful . . . and you could imagine underneath this dress and these
ribbons a statue, and inside this statue a soul.*
— Victor Hugo, Les Misérables

*Women in love are less ashamed than men.
They have less to be ashamed of. —Ambrose Bierce*

What young woman does not want to be beautiful? It is the nature of
Venus to desire to be desired—and there is almost no limit to what some
will do to enhance their beauty. Internationally the cosmetics business is
a forty-five billion dollar industry, nearly half of which is spent in the
United States. And of course, diets, workouts, and cosmetic surgery
supplement the decorative arts. There is both sanity and *insanity* in all of
this. Certainly one should care carefully for their body—it is the temple
of the spirit—and it is a good thing to keep it healthy and attractive. But
true beauty is not found in a bottle, or attained through fad diets, or by
surgically altering the physic. To concern oneself with the outer vessel
only, and not the inner, is vanity—it is allowing polluted water to flow
from a golden faucet.

It is also a common tendency of Venus to envy that which she herself
does not possess—the old "mirror, mirror, on the wall—who's the fairest
of them all" motif. Consider this cameo from Oscar Wilde's play, *An Ideal
Husband:*

MABEL CHILTERN: "What sort of a woman is she?"

LORD GORING: "Oh! A genius in the daytime and a beauty at
night!"

MABEL CHILTERN: "I dislike her already."

Obviously Mabel's response is simply humorous, but it leads us to a serious question—can one envy beauty without diminishing one's own? Does true beauty compete or harmonize? Part of the problem, no doubt is in the definition. What is beauty, this quality that is so essential to our happiness? Emerson said that it is the form in which our minds study the world around us. He further essays:

"All privilege is that of beauty; for there are many beauties . . . Every man values every acquisition he makes in . . . beauty, above his possessions. The most useful man in the most useful world, so long as only commodity was served, would remain unsatisfied. But, as fast as he sees beauty, life acquires a very high value . . . We ascribe beauty to that which is simple; which has no superfluous parts; which exactly answers its end . . . It is the most enduring quality, and the most ascending quality . . . We love any forms from which great qualities shine. If [beauty] exist in the most deformed person, all the accidents that usually displease, please and raise esteem and wonder higher . . . All high beauty has a moral element in it, and the beauty ever in proportion to the depth of thought . . . An adorer of truth we cannot choose but obey, and the woman who has shared with us the moral sentiment, — her locks must appear to us sublime."

Emerson is right on the mark. Our minds are constantly seeking for symmetry, for patterns, for excellence in form. Who can gaze upon the Galaxy Andromeda and not see incomparable beauty? We are not always cognizant of this indefatigable mental search and the unexpected delight, the grand vista which opens suddenly from what was monotonous surroundings, or the discovery of an extraordinary virtue in what was thought to be an ordinary individual—the unexpected delight is always the greater joy.

Beauty cannot be disassociated from Grace. It is the effortless movement of the swan, the kindness of a gentle rain falling on parched ground—love bending to bless. It is friendship to the friendless, intelligence married to modesty. It is the delicate unfolding flower that knows its petals can easily be marred. The Graces were attendants to Aphrodite and Venus, the Love Goddesses of Greece and Rome, daughters of Zeus. They represented loveliness, gentleness, friendship, bloom and brilliance. Their calling was to lift the spirits of gods and men.

Their names were Aglaia, Euphrosyne and Thalia. The ancients thought that no one woman, no matter how divine, could possess all of the graces.

The Graces

The ancients worshiped Graces three.
They could not have considered thee.
Perfect Grace that in thee finds
'Twas unthinkable to their minds.
Aglaia was the nymph of bloom,
Ever young with Spring's perfume.
Brilliant was Euphrosyne,
The cleverest of the coterie.
Thalia was loveliness divine,
Her beauty would intoxicate as wine.
The softer sex did emulate
The Graces, but in mortal state
How could they the gods exceed?
'Though each a virtue may concede.
One was lovely, another kind
Still others blessed with clever mind.
But never could you find all grace
Among the gods or mortal race.
And so it was throughout all time
Until each virtue did combine
In thy small frame and perfect mold.
Astonished are the gods of old!
The Graces are but One, not three!
Each Grace that is, is found in thee!

The realization of such perfection is a heavenly gift bestowed upon that young woman who understands and lives by this truth: ***Beauty is the mark God puts on virtue.***

There is a story in the Apocrypha of a true Beauty. In this instance the author agrees with the Council of Trent, who in 1528 declared that this is a true account and therefore it is scriptural. The scholars of King James excluded it from the Book of Daniel because the only manuscripts then extant were written in Greek, not in the original Hebrew. However, the Council of Trent deduced that the Greek writings were copied from the lost Hebrew text. Interestingly this narrative is entitled *The History of Susanna*. However, it is an account of only one episode in Susanna's life. Normally the *history* of an individual is the story of their entire life. How then does this rightfully qualify as Susanna's history? It will be clear to the reader that the monumental decision Susanna makes in this record reveals that the delicate Susanna is built of granite. What we are made of is proven only by trial; the test, when it comes, discloses our past and foretells our future. Only an event of such magnitude that no forthcoming circumstance could exceed the present terror, would expose where we have been and accurately predict where we are going. Courage is the virtue that proves our depth of commitment to all other virtues. Susanna is given a choice to either compromise her beauty or suffer infamy and death. Therefore it may be truly said that this singular affair is indeed *her history*.

"The History of Susanna

"There dwelt a man in Babylon, called Joacim: And he took a wife, whose name was Susanna, the daughter of Chelcias, a very fair woman, and one that feared the Lord. Her parents also were righteous, and taught their daughter according to the law of Moses."

We learn immediately that Susanna lived during the time of the Babylonian captivity. She was raised in a very religious home by good parents who taught her the great truths which God had revealed to his prophet Moses. Susanna was obedient to God's Law. By contrast there are those persons who believe they are entitled to decide what is right and what is wrong. What a foolish notion! How safe would an airline flight be if the passengers, the majority of whom have no piloting skills and all of whom have no authority to direct flight operations, felt they had the right to decide how the flight should be governed—what altitude should be flown, what deviations in the flight path should be made to circumnavigate severe weather, how the payload should be balanced, what the response should be in an emergency? The truly intelligent are obedient to laws they are not yet capable of understanding. God's laws are eternal truths and we only decide to *choose* to follow His decreed *rights* and shun His decreed *wrongs*—or we choose to disobey His laws. It is never our right to replace His commandments with our own philosophy. If we do we will ultimately discover that the results of such abuse of our free agency will bring upon us utter destruction.

Susanna's understanding of godly truths was not an intellectual or superficial acceptance of them, or the blind obedience of a daughter to her parents' teachings—rather she possessed a deep inner conviction, a personal testimony of God. Her *fear* of the Lord was her preference *towards* Him; she feared to offend God more than she feared to offend man. This type of fear is actually an awe inspired respect, not fraught with horror or panic but composed of the abiding love that a tender daughter feels towards a Father who always requites her love an hundred fold.

Susanna was "very fair." Another translation states she was of "beautiful form." This simplistic description is wonderfully complete. Just as the word *dove* brings immediately to mind a thousand attributes that the word *bird* does not, *fair* is a word reservoir containing within its cistern all of the soul satisfying delights: a complexion light and cool as a spring morning, skin as smooth as fine silk and as soft as a rose petal, a face of delicate symmetry, eyes the color of a clear early evening sky that see only kindness and emanate the goodness of a perfect heart, a pliant and supple mouth whose gentle kiss is as the day's first dew, incapable of slander, hands whose very touch is a healing balm, a mind that refuses to be *open* (for what field of snow is made more fair by dirty refuse)—a mind that refuses to be open save to admit divine truth and inspired *thought*, a cursive fluent form void of vulgarity, yet dramatic in its perfection. Susanna was *very fair.*

> "Now Joacim was a great rich man, and had a fair garden joining unto his house: and to him resorted the Jews; because he was more honourable than all others.
>
> "The same year were appointed two of the ancients of the people to be judges, such as the Lord spake of, that wickedness came from Babylon from ancient judges, who seemed to govern the people. These kept much at Joacim's house: and all that had any suits in law came unto them."

Although a captive in Babylon, Susanna's husband was both great, that is to say influential and respected by his captors as well as his own people, and wealthy. His commodious home was a community center of such renown as to serve as a hall of justice. When legal disputes arose, two judges, long enough in power to grow old as well as corrupt, would try the cases in Joacim's house. These magistrates had so far concealed their lecherous corruption from this most honorable man.

Joacim was a lover of beauty and as he adorned his life with the fair Susanna, he also adorned his home with a fair garden—a flowered and walled sanctuary.

"Now when the people departed away at noon, Susanna went into her husband's garden to walk. And the two elders saw her going in every day, and walking; so that their lust was inflamed toward her. And they perverted their own mind, and turned away their eyes, that they might not look unto heaven, nor remember just judgments. And albeit they both were wounded with her love, yet durst not one shew another his grief. For they were ashamed to declare their lust, that they desired to have to do with her. Yet they watched diligently from day to day to see her."

Susanna enjoyed the peace of solitude. A soul in tune with the Infinite does not seek clamorous society. The Voice of the Spirit is quiescent, mild, diminutive. The Dove broods in our company when we place ourselves in Eden but quickly takes to flight if disturbed by raucous commotion. The Enemy of Joy designs a world filled with a cacophony of voices, a dominion of dissonance, a protectorate of Babel, a world of continual caterwauling. Turn off the radio and TV. Flee the mindless chat rooms on the net, the senseless and endless phone and cell-phone conversations, whose substance is gossip that babels—on and on. Beauty is not willingly found in Babylon.

There is peace also in the comfort of friends whose influence ennobles. But that company who filled Joacim's home to litigate their cases was the antithesis of fellowship. When the crowds disbursed at noon, Susanna sought repose in the garden. A righteous person is never less alone than when all alone. As Childe Harold wrote:

There is beauty in the pathless woods,

There is pleasure on the lonely shore,

There is society where none intrudes,

By the deep sea and music in its roar.

Reality extends far beyond the natural eye and that communion which is *felt* most deeply is most real. During these solitary walks Susanna's pure spirit communed with the Spirit of God. It is in this manner that Beauty receives revelation, quietly and peacefully. Revelation is the unfolding of truth to our understanding through the instrumentality of the Holy Spirit. Those who desire dramatic displays from Heaven do not understand the Lord's methodology. God does not speak thunderously from Mt. Sinai unless we are in a state of rebellion. The Adversary understands these principles and he recognizes that we are most receptive of divine inspiration when we walk reverently in our own Eden. And so he sends forth his emissaries, serpents let loose in the garden whose sole purpose is the destruction of Beauty.

Watchers espied the lovely Susanna as she walked alone in the shade of the flowering trees. Separately the two old judges, unaware of their kindred lust, gazed upon her beauty. At this stage of their evil their consciences evoked a sense of shame in response to their wicked thoughts. However, they were so far advanced in the immoral progression that love and lust, absolute opposites, were confounded as a single passion. Orson F. Whitney wrote:

> "What is love? Can speech define it?
> Love is mightier than language.
> Can the lessor bound the greater?
> Can the brook embrace the ocean?
>
> "Love? Is it but lustful burning,
> Momentary flower of passion?
>
> "Ne'er be day with night confounded,
> Substance mingled with its shadow.
> Lust, the guise of love assuming,
> Wanders forth a homeless beggar,
> Here today, tomorrow yonder;
> Selfish, brutal, bent on taking,
> Savage, groveling and ungrateful."

These elders knew that the law, both of man and God, was in direct opposition to their malicious intent. They shunned the reprimands of conscience and turned away their eyes from heaven. Once the straight course is forsaken and our path is *bent* the last thing we want is to be reminded of the right way. We desire spiritual amnesia—a cloak to cover our plotted and premeditated sin.

> "And the one said to the other, Let us now go home: for it is dinner time. So when they were gone out, they parted the one from the other, and turning back again they came to the same place; and

after that they had asked one another the cause, they acknowledged their lust: then appointed they a time both together, when they might find her alone."

Mob mentality and conspiracy advance the progression of evil. What may be unthinkable transgression to one individually, becomes quite possible when swept along a course by *pseudo* friends; and when one *combines* with others to commit a crime there is a wicked promise of false alibi to prevent punishment. Secret combinations, whether plotted by two or by two hundred, are authored by the same individual who conspired with the serpents in the Genesis garden to destroy Eve—of whom Susanna is a *type*. And like the Mother of all mankind, Susanna in her naiveté, does not recognize the stealthy approach of evil until it is completely upon her. When she realizes her danger she has not even her clothes for a covering of defense. Naked, she is completely exposed to treachery and must choose between defilement or certain death. Thus like Eve her agency is thrust upon her—she is forced to choose and if she chooses *right* she will be shamed in the eyes of her Adam, her own Joacim, by false accusation.

"And it fell out, as they watched a fit time, she went in as before with two maids only, and she was desirous to wash herself in the garden: for it was hot. And there was no body there save the two elders, that had hid themselves, and watched her. Then she said to her maids, Bring me oil and washing balls, and shut the garden doors, that I may wash me. And they did as she bade them, and shut the garden doors, and went out themselves at privy doors . . .[as] she had commanded them: but they saw not the elders, because they were hid."

So modest was Susanna that she desired to cleanse herself without the assistance of her maids. As Susanna bathed herself, the sun bathed the garden in light. The contrast between the afternoon heat and the cool water, the ambiance of aromatic flowers set against an abundance of green foliage, the privacy afforded by the high garden walls, all this must have delighted the senses of the delicate and quiet Susanna. Centuries later the masters Rembrandt , Empoli, Artemsia and Ruben attempted to capture in their paintings the innocence and beauty of this young woman as she washed herself in this natural setting. Sufficient it is to say that the sight of her was too much for the two evil men who had concealed themselves in the dense flora. These Peeping Toms could no longer remain merely voyeuristic. It was impossible for them to see her loveliness as they were blinded by their own lustfulness. For:

"unto them that are defiled and unbelieving [is] nothing pure; but even their mind and conscience is defiled (Titus 1:15)."

How essential is modesty to beauty! Although there is nothing vulgar about the body itself—on the contrary it is in the image of Deity—but it is a foolish and naive young woman who thinks she can display her form in any degree of immodesty without arousing the wicked ardor of those who would think no more of deflowering her virginity than they would to crush a rose bud.

Susanna was not at all to blame—she was guiltless; yet she was soon to face that depravity which should be forever unspeakable—the debasing horror of rape. In her dire circumstance Susanna could not lose her virtue, even if defiled—for virtue can never be robbed, only surrendered. However, unlike Susanna so many young women flit like butterflies around white-flamed torches, inviting tragedy. Instead of concealing their form from the eyes of monsters behind stout walls, they tout their figure with revealing attire. Those guilty of coquetry, whose flirtations and exhibitionism titillate, cannot claim when they are sullied and abused that they are still virtuous. These words are not meant to wound those who have already been deeply wounded—but to awaken the foolish to a sense of their own true beauty before it is lost at the hands of ogres.

"Now when the maids were gone forth, the two elders rose up, and ran unto her, saying, Behold, the garden doors are shut, that no man can see us, and we are in love with thee; therefore consent unto us, and lie with us. If thou wilt not, we will bear witness against thee, that a young man was with thee: and therefore thou didst send away thy maids from thee.

"Then Susanna sighed, and said, I am straitened on every side: for if I do this thing, it is death unto me: and if I do it not I cannot escape your hands."

Susanna possessed a brilliant mind. Immediately she grasped the awfulness of her situation. She saw immediately that there was no escape for her. If she consented to their wickedness she knew that she would suffer a terrible type of internal death; and worst of all a spiritual death, cut off from the sustaining power of the Lord's Spirit. On the other hand, Susanna knew that if she cried out against these despotic judges that her actions could only temporarily save her. These magistrates blatantly threatened that if she did not submit to their debauchery that they would bear false witness against her, charging that she had committed adultery with a young man who, they would lie, fled at their approach. The law stated that a woman accused of adultery by two witnesses would, after dreadful humiliation, suffer a terrible death. Their sham testimony would be her death warrant. How evil progresses! Once these judges had become capable of forcing their immorality upon innocence, they next became capable of shedding innocent blood. To her everlasting honor, as quick as Susanna recognized her plight she as quickly and decisively chose the right! With extraordinary courage she declared:

"It is better for me to fall into your hands, and **not do it**, than to sin in the sight of the Lord. **With that Susanna cried with a loud voice**: and the two elders cried out against her. Then ran the one, and opened the garden door. So when the servants of the house heard the cry in the garden, they rushed in at the privy door, to see what was done unto her.

"But when the elders had declared their matter, the servants were greatly ashamed: for there was never such a report made of Susanna."

How is it that Susanna's own servants were ashamed of their mistress and preferred the testimony of the judges to hers? After all, her reputation was spotless! Beauty is burdened with liabilities. Not only is it envied, it is the object of skepticism—"I knew she was too good to be true" ... "No one can be *that* beautiful and *really* be faithful." It is likely that Joacim was older than Susanna for it is improbable that a young husband could have attained such status and wealth as he enjoyed. The accusers undoubtedly played upon the carnally minded sympathies of the envious by charging that she had been intimate with "a young man." Joacim remains silent to this slander. As the people observed the tacit Joacim, they must have believed that he was deeply wounded by his supposedly unfaithful young wife. Like her servants the entire community, as we shall see, are quick to believe the report of the elders.

"And it came to pass the next day, when the people were assembled to her husband Joacim, the two elders came also full of mischievous imagination against Susanna to put her to death; And said before the people, Send for Susanna, the daughter of Chelcias, Joacim's wife. And so they sent. So she came with her father and mother, her children, and all her kindred."

At her trial her wonderful father, mother and family are at her side, manifesting their confidence in her innocence. Amazingly this has no effect upon the assembly. Why?

> "Now Susanna was a very delicate woman, and beauteous to behold. And these wicked men commanded to uncover her face, (for she was covered) that they might be filled with her beauty. Therefore her friends and all that saw her wept. Then the two elders stood up in the midst of the people, and laid their hands upon her head. And she weeping looked up toward heaven: for her heart trusted in the Lord.

> "And the elders said, As we walked in the garden alone, this woman came in with two maids, and shut the garden doors, and sent the maids away. Then a young man, who there was hid, came unto her, and lay with her. Then we that stood in a corner of the garden, seeing this wickedness, ran unto them. And when we saw them together, the man we could not hold: for he was stronger than we, and opened the door, and leaped out. But having taken this woman, we asked who the young man was, but she would not tell us: these things do we testify.

> "Then the assembly believed them as those that were the elders and judges of the people: so they condemned her to death."

The first argument in the elder's prosecution was to uncover Susanna's veiled face so that the populace might be "filled with her beauty!" As the people gazed upon the "delicate" and youthful splendor of Susanna and compared her appearance to the silent and "honorable" Joacim, and heard with itchy ears the tabloid-like account of how she was found lying with a handsome young man, like Susanna's servants they believed the worst— she was too lovely to be given any benefit of doubt. Her servants did not raise the question how it was that the two elders were in the garden at all, unseen by them when they had left Susanna in seclusion to bathe. Also, as we learn later in the account, these elders had already been guilty of seducing other Israelite women. Although victimized by these vultures, not one of these other women had the courage to come forth and expose the true character of the judges. The influence of her good parents and kindred, her exemplary past, the pitiful tears that flowed from her eyes— all of this had no effect upon the hedonistic assembly. With no Spirit in their judgment, with one voice they allied themselves with their sophisticated and lettered judges and condemned the righteous Susanna to death. No one but God could save her and she appealed to no one but Him:

> "Then Susanna cried out with a loud voice, and said, O everlasting God, that knowest the secrets, and knowest all things before they be: Thou knowest that they have borne false witness against me, and, behold, I must die; whereas I never did such things as these men have maliciously invented against me.

> "And the Lord heard her voice. Therefore when she was led to be put to death, the Lord raised up the holy spirit of a young youth whose name was Daniel . . ."

This was most likely Daniel's prophetic debut. He was not just a young man, but a "young youth." One account states that he was about the same age as was the Christ when he was believed lost by his parents and was found questioning the doctors in the temple. God does not spontaneously direct his interventions. Long before a particular drama is enacted by His servants, they are "raised up" for his purposes:

> "And I raised up of your sons for prophets, and of your young men for Nazarites (Amos 2:11)."

From his infancy Daniel had been prepared by the Lord and had lived worthy to receive His direction. When Susanna was about to be murdered, God spoke through this youth with such authority that the execution is brought to a screeching halt. This brash boy prophet fearlessly condemns not only the judges but calls the men of the assembly "fools!" He *requests* nothing of them, rather he *commands* them to "return to the place of judgement" and he will unveil the truth before them. Daniel is immediately recognized as God-sent, for the men say that God has given him "the honor of an elder" (his young age prohibits the people from bestowing this title). Furthermore Daniel declares that he will cross-examine the judges! Imagine the interest of the assembly as they witness two doctors of law scrutinized legally by a boy of perhaps twelve years of age.

> "Therefore when she was led to be put to death, the Lord raised up the holy spirit of a young youth whose name was Daniel: Who cried with a loud voice, I am clear from the blood of this woman. Then all the people turned them toward him, and said, What mean these words that thou hast spoken? So he standing in the midst of them said, Are ye such fools, ye sons of Israel, that

without examination or knowledge of the truth ye have condemned a daughter of Israel? Return again to the place of judgment: for they have borne false witness against her.

"Wherefore all the people turned again in haste, and the elders said unto him, Come, sit down among us, and shew it us, seeing God hath given thee the honour of an elder. Then said Daniel unto them, Put these two aside one far from another, and I will examine them.

"So when they were put asunder one from another, he called one of them, and said unto him, O thou that art waxen old in wickedness, now thy sins which thou hast committed aforetime are come to light. For thou hast pronounced false judgment and hast condemned the innocent and hast let the guilty go free; albeit the Lord saith, The innocent and righteous shalt thou not slay. Now then, if thou hast seen her, tell me, Under what tree sawest thou them companying together? Who answered, Under a mastick tree. And Daniel said, Very well; thou hast lied against thine own head; for even now the angel of God hath received the sentence of God to cut thee in two.

"So he put him aside, and commanded to bring the other, and said unto him, O thou seed of Chanaan, and not of Juda . . . lust hath perverted thine heart. Thus have ye dealt with the daughters of Israel, and they for fear companied with you: but the daughter of Juda would not abide your wickedness."

To the first judge Daniel revealed that his former sins were now to "come to light." To the second judge Daniel is more direct in his explanation. He declares forthrightly that he has sexually harassed and molested many women, using his position to extort their virtue from them out of *fear*. Thus Daniel lays the foundation of past behavior before the assembly. But of this wickedness Daniel does not delve further. Surely he could have called forth the victims and required their testimony against the iniquitous elders—God knew who these victims were, He had seen their tears, felt their shame and had no doubt heard their prayers; He could have revealed their identity to his young prophet. But in His mercy the Lord does not wound the wounded. Imagine the relief of these women when they saw that Daniel would keep their confidences.

It was not necessary to prove numerous acts of debauchery—this one act of conspiracy and attempted murder was sufficient to invoke capital

117

punishment. Daniel would use their own false testimony against them. Another prophet in another day would declare:

"A man is his own tormentor and his own condemner."

In all of their scheming the corrupt judges had forgotten to mutually agree upon the exact *place* in the garden where the made-up rendezvous was supposed to have occurred.

"Now therefore tell me, Under what tree didst thou take them companying together? Who answered, Under an holm tree. Then said Daniel unto him, Well; thou hast also lied against thine own head: for the angel of God waiteth with the sword to cut thee in two, that he may destroy you.

"With that all the assembly cried out with a loud voice, and praised God, who saveth them that trust in him. And they arose against the two elders, for Daniel had convicted them of false witness by their own mouth: And according to the law of Moses they did unto them in such sort as they maliciously intended to do to their neighbour: and they put them to death. Thus the innocent blood was saved the same day.

"Therefore Chelcias and his wife praised God for their daughter Susanna, with Joacim her husband, and all the kindred, because there was no dishonesty found in her. From that day forth was Daniel had in great reputation in the sight of the people."

Susanna is not only proof that a beautiful wife can also be a faithful wife but her history defines what it is that constitutes true beauty. Abhorring vanity, beauty cares for the inner vessel as well as for the outer. Beauty is not competitive or exclusive. It delights in the accomplishment of others and understands that as there is infinite variety in nature, so also is there in beauty. It is enduring and does not fade with time, yet it is fragile and must be guarded at all costs. It increases with virtue and diminishes quickly with dissipation. When beauty is found where least expected, it is the most wondrous. Coupled with grace, beauty bends to bless, shines with brilliance, and is itself divine loveliness. Beauty is bold courage. It is obedience to order and truth. It cleaves to intelligence and knows its Creator to whom it appeals in times of duress. Beauty is fair, delicate, quiet, modest, grateful, perfect, pliant, natural—yet is dramatic, heroic and stands in sharp contrast against the common background of life. Beauty *sees* but more importantly *feels*. It walks a straight path in

Eden's bower and draws strength from magnificence not her own. Beauty is faithfulness in the face of awful adversity, secure in the confidence of God and assured of His ultimate salvation. What young woman does not want to be beautiful? It is available to all, for as the *History of Susanna* illustrates so very well, beauty is a *choice*.

Bibliography

Primary Sources

Apocrypha, The History of Susanna

Durrant, *The Lessons of History*

Ruskin, John: *Harvard Classics, Volume 28* (P. F. Collier & Son Corporation, New York)

The Scriptures

Jeannette of Domremy

I knew only one Burgundian there and I could have wished his head cut off—however, only if it pleased God. — Jeannette of Domremy

In northeastern France, along the Meuse River and east of the city of Troyes, lies the little village of Domremy. Its name rolls off the tongue musically, like the first three notes of the diatonic scale. More than five centuries ago it was home to a little girl named Jeannette. She was "a good, simple, sweet-natured girl" who was dearly loved, not only by her family, but by the villagers as well. Willingly and cheerfully did she work—in the home with her mother, spinning, sewing and cleaning, and in the outdoors with her father, tending flocks, feeding the animals, and cultivating the earth. She only neglected her labor in the fields when she heard the bells of Notre Dame de Bermont toll for Mass. When Jeannette heard their deep toned peals, her very soul seemed to vibrate within her. She was dexterous and athletic, and would bound fawn-like over the brooks running through the countryside to the parish church. She was so devoted to worship that the other girls and young men would at times make fun of her and tell her she was too pious. Although this would embarrass her, yet it did not change her behavior. Her conduct was in true harmony with her faith for she lived as deeply as she believed. As a young girl and of her own accord she visited and cared for the sick and gave alms to the poor. If she saw that a poor traveler had not a haven to rest when evening approached, she invited the wayfarer to sleep in her bed while she slept beneath the hood of the hearth. The parish priest, Guillaume Front, said that he had never met a better Catholic than Jeannette.

Near Domremy was a tree called the Ladies Tree or the Fairy Tree. Legend claimed that in ancient times a Knight who was Lord of Bourlemont rendezvoused beneath its limbs with a beautiful maiden, a fairy. It was said that it was still a place of enchantment. Each year on *Laetare* Sunday, called "Sunday of the Springs," the young people of the parish had a marvelous outing at the Fairy Tree. There they would picnic and talk, laugh and dance. It may have been on one of these enthralling excursions that a young man of the city of Toul fell in love with Jeanette.

Although she was young, perhaps not more than 15, according to the customs then extant she was of age to marry and the match was favored by her parents. But Jeannette was not of a mind to marry and she told her father that in all things she would be obedient, but not in this. Nonetheless her suitor was so enamoured with her that he claimed she had broken a promise to wed him and sued her for breach of promise. The judge saw through his pretense and after hearing Jeannette's testimony "roundly said that [she] had made the man no promise whatever."

Jeannette's father was deeply troubled by a dream he had concerning her. He told her mother and her brothers that he dreamt that she would leave home and go away with men-at-arms and do great things and suffer intensely. Was his premonition a harbinger of things that would truly come to pass? He anxiously wondered and told his sons, "Truly, if I knew that that must happen which I fear in the matter of my daughter, I had rather you drowned her. And if you did not do it, I would drown her myself." Her father was known as Jacques d'Arc, and after his dream in fact became reality and she left Domremy, she was no longer called Jeannette. She was called, Joan—Joan of Arc.

We sometimes think little of ourselves or we excuse our neglect. We say, "If I don't do it, then someone else will. Others are more qualified. Who am I anyway?" And so we belie the truth that we are *essential*. God gives each of us something critical to accomplish. It does not matter how educated you now are, or what your background is, or how young or old you are. It does not matter if you would rather not do that which you must do. Your errand is vital which means it is a *living* task—it is necessary for the continued existence of something. If you not do it, what happens? The good that should have been dies. For the good that ought to have been cannot be in the *time* that it should have lived. Cannot someone else *eventually* do that which you neglected to do? No one can go back in time and repair an omission (the word itself means not fulfilling a mission). Another person may do something like your undone task but it will be subsequent to your charge and therefore in a different point in time. It will have a life of its' own, for the life of your good will have died in your carelessness. Or—the thing that you were to do or that which you were to save may vanish forever.

Could anyone besides Joan have saved France? Maybe, but not in the time that she saved France—and *France could have died completely without her*. Many nations are now extinct that in their death throes were far less convulsive than the broken kingdom of Charles VII. To begin to comprehend the incredible vitality of Jeanette of Domremy you must understand that Joan knew that she was indispensable. She declared:

> "There is nobody in all the world, neither king nor duke, nor daughter of the King of Scotland, nor any other who can recover the kingdom for France. And there will be no help for the kingdom if not from me. Although I would rather have remained spinning at my mother's side, for it is not my condition, yet must I go and must I do this thing, for my Lord wills that I do so."

Just how lost and dismembered was France when Joan made this prophetic pronouncement? Why could no one else save her country? How is it possible that a young farm maiden could do that which generals and nobles could not do? There is a recurring thematic element that runs through the history of our world; it is the motif of young David saving his country from the Philistines by slaying Goliath. For the Almighty calls "upon the weak things of the world, those who are unlearned and despised, to thrash the nations by the power of [His] Spirit; and their arm [is God's] arm, and [God is] their shield and their buckle." Nowhere in the chronicles of kingdoms is there a more illustrative type of this truth than is found in the story of Joan, deliverer of France.

There was an ancient prophecy, some say that it originated from the oracle Merlin, which was widely known throughout France and England. It said that the Kingdom of France would be lost by a woman and would be saved by a virgin. The woman was Isabel of Bavaria and the virgin was the maid from Domremy. In the fourteenth century *The Hundred Years War* had bled Gaul almost of its sovereignty. But at the later end of the century, France began to recover under the able leadership of Charles V, known as "The Wise." He revived the nobility, glory and spirit of his long besieged realm. On his death his son, Charles VI, ascended to the throne. Charles VI was in nothing like his father and did two infamous things: he married Isabel of Bavaria and he lost his sanity, perhaps not in that order. Tormented with "derangement of intellect" he could not rule and for several years the government was conducted by the Duke of Burgundy. The chief rival of Burgundy was Louis, the Duke of Orleans, brother to the insane Charles. This political enmity became scandalous—Queen

Isabel seduced the Duke of Orleans. The effect of their illicit affair on France was devastating. With the assistance of his mistress the Queen, Louis of Orleans increased in power at the expense of the Duke of Burgundy. A France that had been united under Charles *the Wise* became divided under Queen Isabel into two factions: Burgundy and Orleans. During this time the Queen so completely neglected her mindless husband that the king suffered "an excessive want of cleanliness, sometimes even from hunger."

To keep his sister-in-law, Queen Isabel, in decadent luxury, the Duke of Orleans imposed outrageous taxes. The hard-hit citizens of the capital, the Parisians, thought Louis of Orleans so odious that they refused to recognize his authority and looked instead to the Duke of Burgundy. In 1404 the Duke of Burgundy died, but was succeeded by his son John. John, the new Duke of Burgundy sought absolute power and in 1407 he openly assassinated Louis, Duke of Orleans in the streets of Paris. This murder thrust France into civil war. Opposing John of Burgundy were the royal princes of Orleans, led by Count Armagnac. Initially Queen Isabel sided with the Orleans faction in this war—after all her dead lover had been the Duke of Orleans—that is, until Count Armagnac, of the Orleans party, shut the strumpet out from public affairs and disgraced her by disclosing her many "gallantries." Vindictive, Queen Isabel aligned herself with her lover's murderer, John, Duke of Burgundy. The Queen from Bavaria, with her imbecile husband, now opposed the Royal Family and the nation was deluged in a sea of perils. The dictum that to live by the sword is to die by the sword was fully realized by John of Burgundy, who himself was assassinated. His son Phillip became Duke and continued the intrigue at the infinite cost of France herself.

This protracted civil war did not go unnoticed by the English. Taking advantage of this awful strife the Britons attacked France anew and in the Battle of Azincourt destroyed the nobles of the Orleans party. Of the princes of royal blood, only the young Dauphin, Charles VII remained alive. Queen Isabel, mother of Charles VII, added insult to injury by cruelly taunting him—saying that he was not the descendant of kings but was a bastard.

The House of Burgundy did not suffer at Azincourt. The reason became crystal clear in May of 1420 when the Treaty of Troyes was executed. In the execution of this so-called treaty the lunatic Charles VI was represented by his wife, Queen Isabel of Bavaria, and Phillip, Duke of Burgundy. These two signed the pact as his proxies. Furthermore it was said that Charles VI existed only in a state of unconsciousness and was expected to soon die. The traitorous treaty proclaimed King Henry V of England Regent of France. Furthermore, the articles stated that upon the death of Charles VI, Henry or his heir would succeed as King of France, to the exclusion of the son of Charles VI, Prince Charles VII, the rightful heir to the throne (Charles VII was known as the Dauphin).

And so it was that France was lost by a woman, perfidiously reduced to a province of Britannia, wasted and disfigured by bloodshed and decimated by plague. The only duchy loyal to the Dauphin north of the Loire River was Orleans. It was therefore to the City of Orleans that the English laid siege. South of Orleans the central provinces were less defensible and the Dauphin had virtually no standing army. Not only could Charles VII not afford to pay his troops, he himself was absolutely impoverished and "he had not four crowns" in his treasury. His mother had also stolen his confidence in his right to govern, just as the Burgundians and the English, by his mother's aid, had stolen the north of France. He was not alone in his tremulous fright, for taunting Isabel had robbed the people's spirit and their will for victory. Even the noblemen lost courage. It seemed inevitable that Orleans too would fall. After all, for over one hundred years France had fought unsuccessfully to throw off the yoke of imperialistic England. Now the Queen, allied with Burgundy and with Paris, recognized the English King as the Ruler of France. Record numbers of well-fitted enemy troops occupied Normandy. France was near defeat and could not be saved but by a miracle—and a miracle France would get embodied in the small frame of Joan of Arc.

———————————

"No Testimony is sufficient to establish a miracle, unless the testimony be of such a kind, that its falsehood would be more miraculous . . ."
David Hume

Whenever the supernatural is *truly* made manifest there are always those who attempt to explain away the inexplicable and try to sully the good name of the worker of the miracle. Joan herself did not know her precise age. In the Middle Ages, unless a person was of royal blood, there was no concern about an individual's exact age and there was no need for identity papers. Joan was the legitimate daughter of Jacques d'Arc and his wife Isabelle Romée. Some pseudo-historians have tried to fix her birth in the year 1407 and have wrongly surmised that she was a bastard child of Queen Isabel and the Duke of Orleans—the year 1407 was the last year of the romantic liaison between Isabel and Orleans. This false charge would make Joan half-sister to the Dauphin and is an attempt to establish a conspiracy between Joan and Charles VII. Such a conjecture is ridiculous and in no way explains Joan's astounding victories over the English. Had she been born in 1407 she would have been twenty-five at the time of her *Trial of Condemnation*. Rather, Joan and a vast number of witnesses testified that she was "nineteen or thereabouts." There is a tremendous difference between a girl in her late teens and a woman in her mid-twenties, which would not have been overlooked by her judges. Many who gave testimony in the trial knew her as a child, and knew that she was the goodly daughter of Jacques d'Arc, and knew her age to be approximately nineteen, placing the year of her birth at 1412.

In 1425 Joan received her first revelation.

"When I was thirteen years old, I had a voice from God to help me govern my conduct. And the first time I was very fearful. And came this voice, about the hour of noon, in the summer-time, in my father's garden . . . [a] brightness [came] from the same side as the voice . . . a great light."

Joan's revelations are often referred to as her "voices," plural. This is an accurate generalization for she was instructed by the voice of the Lord, and also by the mouths of three angelic servants of Christ—Michael, Catherine and Margaret. However, they not only spoke to her, but they also bodily appeared to her. These three angels became her mentors and in the space of four years prepared her to accomplish her astounding military victories.

"Saint Michael, when he came to me, told me that Saint Catherine and Saint Margaret would come to me and that I should act by their advice, that they were bidden to lead me in what I had to do and that I should believe in what they would say to me and that it was by God's order. The first time I was a child and was afraid. . . . He told me to be a good child and that God would help me. And, among other things he told me to come to the help of the King of France. . . . And the Angel told me the pitiful state that was in the Kingdom of France."

Joan's description of their appearance fills the heart with reverence and are reminiscent of Apostle John's experience when he saw an angel of God on the Isle of Patmos. Neither description includes the misconception of angelic wings, for such are only symbols.

"He, [Michael], was in the form of a true and honest man . . . As for [Michael and the other angels], I saw them with my own eyes . . . I believe as firmly the doings and sayings of St. Michael who appeared to me as I believe that our Lord Jesus Christ suffered death and passion for us. And what moves me to believe this is the good advice, the good comfort and the good doctrine that he did and gave me.

" . . . I embraced both [Catherine and Margaret]. I could not embrace them without feeling and touching them . . . I made them my reverence, for I know well that they are of those who are of the kingdom of paradise.

". . . Before the raising of the siege of Orleans and since, every day, when they speak to me, they have often called me 'Joan the Maid, daughter of God.'"

Of the many truths that she was taught, none was more important than her relationship to Deity. And when her Lord spoke directly to her, He said, "Daughter-God (*Fille-Dé*), go, go, go, I shall be at your aid, go."

So pure was Joan that it seemed the "veil was taken from her mind and the eyes of her understanding were opened" continually.

"[The angels of God] often come among Christian people and are not seen. I have seen them many times among Christians."

In October of 1428 the English laid siege to the City of Orleans. Using great canons that fired 80 pound stones, the British destroyed twelve mills along the River Loire, assaulting and taking possession of the blockhouses that were the cities outward defenses. They also gained control of the bridge that crossed the Loire River to the Tourelles fortification. This vital bridge was the only connection between Orleans and that part of France still loyal to Charles VII. Thus the walled City of Orleans was cut off and besieged by the English who knew that sooner or later famine would conquer the French forces and the people within. The siege continued for months with convoys of food and troop reinforcements bolstering the English while the people of Orleans saw their sustenance diminish daily. Several times the brave French soldiers would sally forth in hopes of gaining some advantage over their enemies or capture much needed food. But the results of their desperate ventures were often disastrous. The last such endeavor was on February 12, 1429, known as the "day of the herrings." The French unsuccessfully attempted to seize a convoy of salt herring and suffered tremendous losses without obtaining so much as an ounce of food.

A month earlier, in January of 1429, Joan quietly left her home in Domremy for the nearby town of Vaucouleurs. Her entire mission had now been revealed to her. She was not only to "help" the Dauphin, but this seventeen year old girl was commanded to raise the siege of Orleans, and clear the northern cities of the English and Burgundians all the way to the City of Reims—historically the site of the coronation of the Kings of France. Joan was to personally see to it that the Dauphin, Charles VII, was crowned King of France at Reims. Knowing of the great pain her leaving would cause her family, and fearing that her father might forbid her departure, she did not tell them. Several years later at her trial she was asked, "When you left your father and your mother, did you think you were committing a sin?" Her response discloses her absolute conviction to her cause:

> "Since God commanded it, it had to be. Since God commanded it, had I had a hundred fathers and a hundred mothers, had I been a King's daughter, I should have departed.
>
> ". . . I went to my uncle's and I told him that I wanted to stay with him for a time and there I stayed about eight days. And I then told my uncle that I must go to the town of Vaucouleurs and my uncle took me there."

In this town Joan called upon Lord Robert de Baudricourt to provide her an escort to travel to the Chateau of Chinon, there to meet with Charles VII. She was bold as to her purpose but he twice rejected her and treated her as one might expect a man of proud blood to treat a peasant. For three weeks she lodged at the home of Catherine Le Royer and openly declared her mission. Along with many of the townspeople Joan won over Catherine Le Royer to her cause. Years later this same Catherine of Vaucouleurs testified:

> "It was then that [Joan] sent to have speech with the lord Robert de Baudricourt that he take her to the place where the Dauphin was. But the lord Robert would not. And when Joan saw that

Robert would not take her, she said: 'Have you not heard it said that it has been prophesied that France shall be lost by a woman and restored by a virgin from the Lorraine marches?' I remembered having heard that and I was stupefied. Joan ardently desired this and the time lagged for her as for a woman pregnant of a child until the time when she would be taken to the Dauphin. And after that I believed in her words and with me many others . . ."

Catherine's husband, Henri Le Royer stated:

"Joan said that she must make her way to the noble Dauphin, for her Lord, the King of Heaven, wished her to go there and the King of Heaven was thus her sponsor; that though she be obliged to make her way there on her knees, go she would."

Squire Jean de Metz tells of his first meeting with Joan and of his conversion to her holy purpose:

"When Joan the Maid came to the place and town of Vaucouleurs I saw her, dressed in poor clothes, women's clothes . . . I spoke to her, saying, 'My dear girl, what are you doing here?' and the Maid answered me, 'I am come here to talk with Robert de Baudricourt, but he pays no attention to me nor to my words. And yet, before we are in mid-Lent, I must be at the King's side . . . for my Lord wills that I do so.' I asked her who was her Lord. And she told me that it was God. Whereupon I, Jean, who bear witness here, promised the Maid, putting my hand in hers in a gesture of good faith, that God helping, I would lead her to the King."

Most likely Jean de Metz, who ranked next below a knight in feudal hierarchy, influenced Lord Baudricourt to grant Joan an audience. Baudricourt must have been astounded by Joan's direct and authoritative manner of speaking. She said to him:

"The Kingdom of France is not the Dauphin's but my Lord's. But my Lord wills that the Dauphin shall be made King and have the Kingdom in custody. The Dauphin shall be King despite his enemies, and I shall lead him to his anointing."

This third petition of Joan's was granted and Squire Jean de Metz, Bertrand de Poulengy and two of his servants conducted her to the Prince. This was a very dangerous time to journey to Chinon for there were "men-at-arms everywhere." But Joan inspired her four escorts with courage saying, "God would clear the way for her to go to the lord Dauphin, and that she had been born to do this." For eleven days they traveled, often at night for fear of the Burgundians and the English. When they stopped to sleep, Joan would lay between her two chief guards, Jean and Bertrand. Her beauty and her passion in the cause of France evoked great admiration from her companions. Later they both testified that her conduct was impeccable. Said Jean de Metz:

> "I was fired by her sayings and with love for her, divine as I believe. I believe that she was sent by God . . .

> "On our way, Bertrand and I, we lay down with her, and the Maid lay beside me, keeping on her doublet and hose; and I [respected] her so that I would never have dared make advances to her . . ."

On the fifth month of the siege of Orleans, on February 23, 1429 Joan of Arc arrived in Chinon for her foreordained meeting with the Dauphin, Charles VII. She was not granted an immediate audience with Charles and he deliberated with his counselors whether or not he should hear her. The advisors to the Dauphin, who were clerks and clergymen, proposed to Joan that she relay her message to Charles through them. She would not hear of this and said that she would speak in detail only to the Prince. But she did say that she had come with a mandate from the King of Heaven to accomplish two purposes: one, to raise the siege of Orleans; and two, to lead the Dauphin to Reims to be crowned King of all France. Charles was advised not to see her by these courtiers and he was so inclined, until he learned that Lord "Robert de Baudricourt had written to him that he was sending him a woman and that she had been conducted through the territory of the [his] enemies; and that, in a manner quasi-miraculous, she had crossed many rivers by their fords, to reach [him]." Still, he was leery of this young maid from Domremy who made such fabulous claims. And so when she was admitted into the great of hall of the Chateau of Chinon, Charles "withdrew apart from the others" and in a manner of speaking, hid himself from Joan. She was therefore not *brought before* her Sovereign nor was she introduced to him. There was also nothing in his dress or manner to disclose his identity to Joan. The Dauphin was to witness his first preternatural encounter with Joan. She looked among the many present and quickly singled him out as her Prince. She said:

> "I knew him among the others by the counsel of my voice which revealed him to me."

She greeted him in such a manner that all present were struck with amazement:

"Gentle Dauphin, Joan the Maid is my name, and to you is sent word by me from the King of Heaven that you will be anointed and crowned in the town of Reims and you will be Lieutenant to the King of Heaven who is King of France."

Yet her noble salutation far from convinced Charles and his court that she was indeed so commissioned from God. What persuaded him that Joan was Heaven-sent and not a lunatic? It should be remembered that Isabelle of Bavaria had mocked her son with derision causing him to be uncertain whether he was indeed the son of Charles VI. In his heart he wondered if he truly was the heir to the throne of France. Though he kept these doubts hidden from his court, yet he certainly lacked the confidence to act as a king. Joan requested that he meet with her in private and there she gave him a *sign* that caused him to begin to believe in her mission and in his own right to rule. For years, no one knew what the sign was that Joan gave him. Later in her trial she firmly refused to disclose what she revealed to her Dauphin that day in Chateau Chinon. It was not until after the death of Charles that his chamberlain, Guillaume Gouffier, divulged the secret of the sign from Joan of Arc to the chronicler Pierre Sala. Sala wrote:

"He told me the secret which had been between the King and the Maid . . . In the time of the great adversity of Charles VII, he found himself brought so low that he no longer knew what to do. . . . being in this extremity, [he] entered one morning alone into his oratory and there he made a humble petition and prayer to Our Lord in his heart, without utterance of words, in which he petitioned devoutly that if so it was that he was true heir descended from the noble House of France and that the kingdom should rightly belong to him, that it please Him to keep and defend him, or, at worst, to grant him the mercy of escaping death or prison. . . .A little time afterwards, it came about that the Maid was brought to him . . . and there she gave her message at the sign aforesaid (of his petition that only God and he had knowledge of) which [Charles] knew to be true. And thenceforth he took counsel of her."

In Joan's own words she declared to Charles:

"I tell thee, on behalf of Messiah, that thou art true heir to France and King's son, and He has sent me to thee to lead thee to Reims, that thou mayst receive thy coronation and thy consecration."

No one had heard Charles utter his prayer to God—as he formed the words in his mind and prayed from his heart. Yet this little maid knew of this private supplication and brought him God's answer to his prayer. She affirmed that he was the "true heir," the legitimate Sovereign of France. He would not suffer the defeat of death or imprisonment, his secret fear. Rather, he would be led to Reims, the place where his progenitors had been crowned, and there he would receive his own coronation.

Charles, although deeply shaken by the sign she had given him, still wanted to be as certain as he could possibly be that Joan's knowledge came from God and was not some act of witchcraft. In any case, it would require a huge leap of faith in any age or circumstance to entrust veteran soldiers to an unlearned farm girl. Thus she was taken to Poitiers to be interrogated by the clergy who were charged with the responsibility of validating her character and her divine commission. This was her first "trial." She was examined to see if she was a virgin, an indication in the eyes of her judges that she had dedicated her life to God, and was found to be a true maid of virtue. She was asked many questions of these masters of theology. Of this period Jean Pasquerel stated:

> "[Joan] was not pleased with all these interrogations and [said] that they were preventing her from accomplishing the work for which she was sent and that the need and time were come to act."

The course of this trial is best understood in brevity by relating some of Joan's answers to her jurists.

> "For three weeks I was examined by learned men in Chinon and Poitiers . . .

> "In God's name, let us go on!

> "I am come from the King of Heaven to raise the siege of Orleans and to lead the Dauphin to Reims to be crowned and annointed.

> "In God's name, I did not come to Poitiers to give signs! Take me to Orleans, and I will show you a sign and for what I am sent.

> "The Voice has told me that it is God's will to deliver the people of France from the calamity that is upon them.

(She is asked, "If it be God's will to deliver them, then there is no need for soldiers," to which she answers): "The soldiers will fight, and God will give the victory!"

At the conclusion of this examination her judges reported to the Dauphin that "they had found nothing but what was good in her . . . nothing in her contrary to the Catholic faith and that considering his necessity, the [Dauphin] could make use of her to help him." She was thus empowered by Charles to take provisions and a number of soldiers to Orleans. She was not made the commander of all the army, or *chef de guerre* (war chief), but was appointed a captain, equal to the other captains under the supreme authority of Count Dunois, known as the Bastard of Orleans. Joan had an *ensign* made on "which was painted the image of Our Savior seated in judgment in the clouds."

"I bore this standard when we went forward against the enemy to avoid killing anyone. I have never killed anyone."

Charles gave her a suit of armor "proper to her body." Buried beneath the altar in the church of Saint Catherine at Fierbois she unearthed a rusted sword, which when polished gleamed like her armor. So dressed as a knight she mounted her horse as if she had been born upon its back, and with the banner of her Lord she rode fearlessly with her convoy of men and food for the besieged city of Orleans.

Imagine, if you will, the hauteur of the English as they looked down upon nearly conquered France. The capital city of Paris had acknowledged the British Crown as her Lord, as had all the cities north of the Loire—with the exception of Orleans. This last bastion of the French nationals, cut off now for six months, was certain to fall in a matter of weeks. With its destruction they could sweep into the Central Provinces without fear of an attack on their rear guard and with little opposition on their front. English victory, although not quite yet attained, was absolutely assured. Then came word that a small force from Chinon, led by a teen-age maiden, was marching to Orleans to give them battle. It was preposterous news, made more so by an ultimatum they received from this maid commander calling for their immediate surrender and withdrawal, not only from Orleans, but from all of France! Certainly they held this dispatch in derision—yet this was less like a threat and more like a decree. It read:

"King of England, and you, Duke of Bedford, who call yourself Regent of the Kingdom of France; you, William de la Pole, Earl of Suffolk; John, Lord Talbot; and you, Thomas, Lord Scales, who call yourselves lieutenants of the said Duke of Bedford: Do justice to the King of Heaven; surrender to the Maid, who is sent here from God, King of Heaven, the keys of all the good towns you have taken and violated in France. She is come from God to uphold the blood royal. She is ready to make peace if you will do justice, relinquishing France and paying for what you have withheld.

"As to you, you archers and men-at-arms, gentle and others, who are before the town of Orleans, go hence into your own country in God's name; and if you do not so, expect to hear news of the Maid, who will shortly come to see you, to your very great damage.

"King of England, if you do not so, I am a commander, and in whatever place in France I come upon your men, I will make them leave it . . . and if they will not yield obedience, I will have them all slain. I am sent here from God, King of Heaven, to put you, hand to hand, out of all France. Yet if they will yield obedience, I will grant them mercy.

"And think not otherwise: for you shall not hold the Kingdom of France from God, King of Heaven, Saint Mary's son, but King Charles shall hold it, the true heir. For so God, King of Heaven, wills it; and so it has been revealed to him by the Maid, and he shall enter Paris with a fair company.

"If you will not believe this news from God and the Maid, wherever we find you, there we shall strike; and we shall raise such a battle-cry as there has not been in France in a thousand years, if you will not do justice. And know surely that the King of Heaven will send more strength to the Maid than you can bring against her and her good soldiers in any assault. And when the blows begin, it shall be seen whose right is the better before the God of Heaven.

"You, Duke of Bedford: The Maid prays and beseeches you not to bring on your own destruction. If you will do her justice, you may yet come in her company . . . So answer if you will make peace in the city of Orleans. And if you do not so, consider your great danger speedily.

"Written this Tuesday in Holy Week, March 22, 1429."

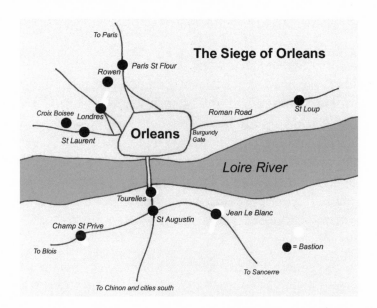

The Siege of Orleans

To Paris
Rowen
Paris St Flour
Croix Boisee
Londres
Roman Road
St Loup
St Laurent
Orleans
Burgundy Gate
Loire River
Tourelles
St Augustin
Jean Le Blanc
Champ St Prive
To Blois
= Bastion
To Sancerre
To Chinon and cities south

Their reaction to Joan was insult. They slurred her innocent name calling her "whore." However, when the news of her coming reached the ears of the famine stricken people of Orleans, they were of the opposite opinion, believing that her coming was an answer to their prayers. When Joan approached Orleans the French soldiers went out with great zeal to skirmish with the English and create many diversions so that she might safely enter into the city with her desperately needed supplies. Count Dunois, the Commander of Orleans, with his knights, rode out to meet her and reinforce her entry—but he was greatly concerned. To get her men, the bales of wheat, the sheep, pigs and cows past the English and into the city would require bypassing the English-held roads. The only other route was the river Loire, however impossible. Requisitioning boats and building rafts, which were loaded with this immense cargo, Joan sailed up the river Loire against the current and into the wind, an unimaginable task!

It is interesting to note that when Joan met with Count Dunois, she was not so much interested in supplying the city as she was in commencing the fight. She believed that the sooner she gave battle the sooner she would conquer! When Dunois tried to "counsel" Joan she responded that her counsel was better than his, as she received it from heaven. At that moment the wind changed and blew with such strength as to enable them to embark upon the Loire upstream to Orleans and they safely entered the city despite the English. This change of fortune amazed Dunois. He was to find that Joan was to astonish him far more in the coming days.

Having slipped past their enemies the French disembarked near the eastern gate of the city. It was Friday, April 29, 1429, at 8:00 in the evening. Joan mounted her white horse, and bearing her standard of Christ, rode at the head of her convoy bringing life and relief into the city of Orleans. Her equestrian skill was such that the citizens marveled and led them to declare that it was as though "she had long served in the wars." She was met by the "burgesses and matrons of Orleans, bearing great plenty of torches and making such rejoicing as if they had seen God descend in their midst . . . they felt themselves no longer besieged, by the divine virtue . . . who looked upon them all affectionately, whether men, women, or little children." There was a great "press to touch her or the horse upon which she was."

Again, the general of all the French Forces at Orleans was Dunois. Joan was appointed as one of his many captains. On the following morning, Joan was eager to engage the enemy, but Dunois and the other captains were united in their strategy to wait. They were of the opinion that their forces were not sufficiently strong and that they had to be further reinforced. Saturday, Sunday, Monday, and Tuesday were spent in this awful waiting. It was known that the English were also awaiting reinforcements from Falstaff. On Wednesday, May 4th, Joan angrily accosted Dunois, telling him that he must apprise her of Falstaff's progress and include her in his council. If not, Joan simply announced:

"I promise thee I will have thy head taken off!"

After this argument with her commander, Joan was greatly wearied and retired to her chamber to rest. Suddenly she awoke and cried out to Louis de Coutes, "Ah—you told me not that the blood of France was spilling!" She had just received a revelation that a skirmish was being fought outside of the city near the Bastion of Saint-Loup and her countrymen were in great need. Quickly she put on her armor and commanded that de Coutes saddle and bridle her horse. She wasted no time with Dunois, but so swiftly mounted her white charger that her attendant had to pass her standard out to her through a window. Then she was off, not looking to see who followed her into battle. She galloped through the Burgundy gate and down the Roman road towards Saint-Loup. The sight of "many wounded French saddened her." But as soon as the soldiers of France saw her ride forth in fury, her *ensign* unfurled and streaming in the wind, they rallied manfully and surged as a mighty wave against their foes. The Fortress of Saint-Loup was taken and many English men-at-war were killed.

Joan then exhorted her men to "confess their sins and to give thanks to God for the victory won." It is one thing for men to fight a common external enemy. It is quite another to motivate individuals to personally fight the enemy within themselves. At this pivotal moment when the French soldiers knew in their hearts that the fortunes of war were beginning to be divinely redirected through the agency of this young heroine, but also knowing that a complete victory was a formidable if not nearly an impossible task, Joan boldly declared to her men that France had previously lost to her enemies because of the sin of immorality! And not just for the sins of their Queen Isabel—they had lost because of their own sexual misconduct. She commanded the soldiers:

"Take care that women of ill-fame follow not the army, for it was for those sins that God allowed the war to be lost."

She then prophesied that if they were faithful:

"Within five days the siege of Orleans would be raised and there would linger no more English before the city."

Dunois and his captains were certainly pleased with Joan's victory at Saint-Loup but felt, having attained this advantage, future engagements should be taken with greater caution. Lord de Gaucourt was charged to guard the gates so that Joan should not again instigate a major attack without the command of Dunois. Joan was "ill-content" with this censure, and once again took matters into her own hands. She sent a second, and then a third ultimatum to the British, but predictably to no avail. On Friday, May 6th, Joan rallied a considerable force of men, more it appears, than her own command. She ordered Lord de Gaucourt out of her way and told him that he "was a bad man." Seeing himself in peril, de Gaucourt removed his guard from the gate. Joan and her men left the city and crossed the Loire River by boat. As they approached the blockhouse of Saint Jean Le Blanc the English retreated to the heavily fortified Bastion of Saint Augustin. There was some "disorder" among the French who believed they were not strong enough to attack Augustin. In this confusion the English opened the gates of the Fortress Saint Augustin to take the offensive and attack the bemused French. Joan immediately saw the danger of this disarray. She whirled her white horse towards the Bastion of Saint Augustin, and with battle shout, lowered her banner as a lance and rode directly into the attacking English. Her courageous charge had an immediate effect upon her men who bravely followed her in the strength of their might. They assailed their enemies who retreated into Saint Augustin. This retreat of the English and Burgundians back within the walls of the bastion would not save them. The French, who only moments before were disordered, now fought with inspired confidence and singleness of purpose; under the banner of Joan d'Arc they stormed the bastion with incredible spirit and prevailed.

Strategically this victory was critical, for the Fortress of Saint Augustin covered the fortification of Tourelles. Tourelles stood at the end of the bridge that crossed over the Loire into the City of Orleans. If Tourelles and the bridge between it and Orleans were taken, the city would again have direct access to the rest of France. Nonetheless, a council was held and while great appreciation was shown Joan for her tremendous feat, she was told that "they were but few by comparison with the English" and that *now* they must wait upon the Dauphin for more troops. Joan responded:

> "You have been at your counsel and I at mine; and know that my Lord's counsel will be accomplished and will prevail and that [your] counsel will perish."

She then told her aid:

> "Rise tomorrow early in the morning . . . and be always at my side, for tomorrow I shall have much to do, and more than I ever had, and *tomorrow the blood will flow out of my body above my breast.*"

On Saturday, May 7th, Joan ignored Dunois and his captains, and led the French in battle against Tourelles and the bridge that spanned the Loire. The assault was fierce, the advantage being heavy on the side of the English, with many being slain on both sides. Joan led the foray— exposing herself, as she always did, to great danger. Suddenly an archer let fly an arrow, which pierced her body above her breast. She fell wounded and moaned in great pain. Some of the soldiers in pity for her wanted to apply a "charm" to the tear in her body. Although she wept she would not allow any sorcery and told them:

> "I would rather die than do a thing which I know to be a sin or against the will of God."

Joan was carried from the field of battle. Her wound was serious and was dressed with olive oil. All day long the French fought while Joan convalesced. Without hope of victory, Dunois was about to break off the battle at nightfall when the injured Joan, having risen from her bed, approached him. The fact that she could even walk after receiving such a serious blow was amazing, but before the night was over she would astound Dunois, his fighters and their enemies. He relates:

"Then came the Maid to me and required me to wait yet a while. She herself mounted her horse and retired alone into a vineyard, some distance from the crowd of men. And in this vineyard she remained at prayer during one half of a quarter of an hour. Then she came back from that place, at once seized her standard in hand and placed herself on the parapet of the trench, and the moment she was there the English trembled and were terrified."

Joan cried out to the English commander, Captain Classidas, who held the bridge:

"Classidas, Classidas, yield thee, yield thee to the King of Heaven; thou hast called me 'whore', me; I take great pity on thy soul and thy people's!'"

The French were awe inspired by this incredible young woman of valor. They fought as if the victory were already theirs. Suddenly the English could resist no longer and begin to flee across the boulevard of the bridge towards the Tourelles fortification—but the rush of the divinely empowered French was too great and five hundred of the English were killed, either by the sword or by drowning. Captain Classidas fell from the bridge into the Loire and being heavily armored was himself drowned. Joan knowing that these men had lost more than their mortal lives wept in pity for her slain enemies. The French pursued their advantage and soon the bastion of Tourelles was taken by them. Orleans was no longer cut off—the French had secured their east flank, and most importantly they had opened the road to the south across the Loire Bridge. The English still occupied the western and northern fortifications.

The following morning was Sunday, May 8, 1429. Joan commanded the French soldiers and the people of Orleans to repent of their sins and to pray to God for victory. She then ordered her men-in-battle upon the plains outside of the city walls directly opposing the ranks of their enemies. She commanded that "for love and honor of the holy Sunday, they begin not the battle nor make assault on the English; but if the English attacked, let them defend themselves strongly and boldly and have no fear, and they would be the masters."

For one hour the two armies faced each other without so much as a single whistle of an arrow from an archer's hand. Then, unexpectedly, the English turned about and swiftly left the field! The siege of Orleans, begun on the twelfth day of October, 1428, was raised! The French captured "great bombards, and canon, bows, cross-bows, and other artillery" from the retreating British army. Joan the Maid re-entered the City of Orleans to the shouts of the people, exulting and rejoicing in their deliverance and praising God for their victory! Chartier writes:

> "Here is she who seems not to issue from any place on earth, but rather sent by Heaven to sustain with head and shoulders a France fallen to the ground. O astonishing virgin! Worthy of all fame, of all praise, worthy of all the divine honors! Thou art the honor of the reign, thou art the light of the lily, thou art the splendor, the glory, not only of Gaul (France) but of all Christians. Let Troy celebrate her Hector, let Greece pride herself upon Alexander, Africa upon Hannibal, Italy upon Caesar and all the Roman generals. France . . . may well content herself with this Maid only . . . She [is] . . . above them."

The triumph of Orleans was the rebirth of the spirit of France. True it was that the English still occupied all of the villages and castles north of the Loire and their defeat at Orleans by no means marked the end of the war. In fact, it would be another eight years before Charles would recover the capital city of Paris. But the French victory in this city besieged for seven months was far more than a turning point in the war—it was far more than spectacular—it was a true miracle! God, through the instrumentality of Joan the Maid, had shown the nobles, the clergy, the soldiers, and the peasants that he wanted France to be free from imperialistic British rule. God had shown that He would intercede on their behalf and what His terms would be for his intervention. He required their faith, their hope, and their prayers and He required that they not compromise themselves with evil. He required, as Joan had said, that they fight manfully and He would give the victory. Orleans was a baptism—the death of the old disjointed France and the natal beginning of a new united France awakened to liberty. The metaphor of birth implies growth, learning, development—all before maturity and wisdom. After Orleans, the Dauphin was still not King and

France was still not free. But from the liberated Bastions of Orleans a spirit flew forth upon the winds of change, broad over Gaul. Into some hearts it swept as the fire of Pentecost. Others, dull from the tenuous years of subjugation or callused by intrigue, did not receive this spirit when first it eddied around them. But its power and warmth ultimately penetrated even these hearts. Soul by soul and village by village was roused to walk in newness of hope. This rebirth began the process of the erudition required of an independent people.

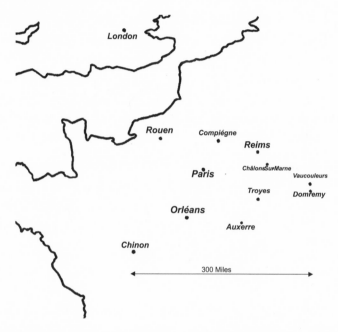

Joan had prophesied of a whole, free and cohesive France, and certainly had hopes of living to see her country flourish under Charles. But she had not promised that she herself would lead France to the final victory—only that she had "come from the King of Heaven to raise the siege of Orleans and to lead the Dauphin to Reims to be crowned." The first she had achieved, the second she must accomplish with all expediency. Perhaps she sensed that her life would be short. She said she feared nothing but treachery—a statement that foreshadowed the actual cause of her death. She knew there was a *time* appointed for her to fulfill her vital mission, and that *time* must not be violated. Predictably, among the nobles, she was nearly alone in this feeling of urgency.

Joan met with Charles on May 9, 1429, the day after her conquest, and although he was sincerely filled with joy at her sudden and unexpected success, he did not authorize her immediately to march onward and take the offensive against the English. Instead Charles convened a number of councils. Joan beseeched him and the French Captains:

> "Noble Dauphin, hold no more so many and such long councils, but come as quickly as you can to Reims to take the crown.

> "Fear not, however many they be! Neither weigh difficulties. God guides our work. Were I not certain that God guides this work, I would rather keep sheep than expose myself to such perils.

> "In God's name! We must fight them. Did they hang from the clouds we should have them! For God is sending them to us . . . and we shall have the greatest victory . . . My council has told me that they are all ours.

> "We must go to Reims. When once the King is crowned and anointed, his enemies' strength will steadily grow less, and finally they will have no power to harm him or the Kingdom.

> "I have no fear for lack of men. There will [be] many to follow."

The French chronicler Regine Pernoud writes:

> "It was Joan who forced them to a decision while they were hesitating which way to go and opinions in Council were diverse, she it was, as all the documents prove, who carried her point and so got the royal army away to Reims, with the object of crowning the King.

> "Meanwhile that army had been enlarged by an accretion of volunteers. And throughout the whole course of the Loire campaign, which was to take the army to Reims, this 'snowball' effect continued."

Just as Joan inspired the French she frightened the English. Jean de Wavrin wrote:

> "By the renown of Joan the Maid the courage of the English was much impaired and fallen off. They saw, it seemed to them, their fortune turn its wheel sharply against them . . . they saw their men stricken down and did not now find them . . . so firm and prudent."

On the 12th of June the city of Jargeau was won by Joan. In this battle Joan was again hurt, struck by a stone which shattered on her helmet, knocking her off the scaling ladder to the ground. But she rose to her feet and exclaimed:

"Friends, friends, up, our Lord has condemned the English, in this hour they are ours, be of good heart."

Before the hour was up she defeated her enemies. Over a thousand English were slain in the battle of Jargeau. On the 15th of June she took Meung back from the British. On June 17th Beaugeny fell to the French. On June 18th Joan was victorious at Patay. On June 25th Joan wrote:

"To the loyal Frenchmen of Tournai —

Noble loyal Frenchmen of Tournai town, the Maid sends you news from these parts: that in one week she has chased the English out of all the places that they held along the River Loire, either by assault or otherwise, in which encounters many English were killed and captured, and she has routed them in a pitched battle. Know too that the Earl of Suffolk, his brother La Pole, Lord Talbot, Lord Scales, with Sir John Fastolf and many other knights and captains have been captured, and a brother of the Earl of Suffolk's and Glasdale were killed.

"Keep yourselves loyal Frenchmen, I pray you. I pray you too and beg you to be ready, all of you, to come to the anointing of noble King Charles at Reims, where we shall shortly be. And come out to meet us when you hear that we are near. I commend you to God. God keep you and give you grace to maintain the good cause of the Kingdom of France."

After so many victories, which finally assured the Dauphin, Charles VII that the Maid would prove true to her word, on June 29th he joined the royal army in their march to Reims. On June 30th the town of Auxerre changed their allegiance to Charles without a battle. On the 5th of July Joan's march halted on the outskirts of Troyes, the very city where Burgundy and the harlot Queen had committed treason, signing that reprehensible treaty which intended to disinherit the Dauphin, Charles VII, and enthrone the King of England over France.

The citizens of Troyes, knowing that they were well armed, walled and defended, were so bold as to openly declare that they would remain loyal to the Duke of Burgundy and King Henry of England. The Dauphin fell again to doubt. Dunois writes:

"Before the city of Troyes [Charles VII] held council with the lords of his blood and the other captains of war to consider whether they should set themselves before the city and lay siege to it or take it, or if it would be better to *march past it*, and going directly to Reims and leaving this city of Troyes. The King's council was divided between diverse opinions and they wondered what was best to be done. Then the Maid came and entered into the council and spoke these words or nearly: 'Noble Dauphin, order that your people go and besiege the town of Troyes and stay no longer in council, for, in God's name, within three days I will take you into the city Troyes by love or by force or by courage, and false Burgundy will stand amazed.' Then the Maid crossed at once with the King's army and left the encampment beside the moats, and made admirable dispositions (she ordered the moats to be filled with bundles of wood and the inhabitants began to greatly fear the coming attack). . . she worked so well that night that on the morrow the bishop and the citizens of the city made their obedience to the King, shaking and trembling."

It was on the 12th of July that Troyes swore their fealty to Charles followed in like manner by the citizens of Châlons-Sur-Marne on 14th of July. Only one city more could prove an obstacle to the coronation of the Dauphin—the city of Reims itself. Charles expressed his fear that Reims would resist his entry and he had not the means, the artillery or war machines, to properly lay siege. Simon Charles wrote:

"Joan told the [Dauphin] to advance boldly and to fear nothing, for if he would advance courageously he would recover all his kingdom."

Charles did exactly as Joan had so advised and on the 16th of July he entered the historic city of Reims to the accolades of the gentry and the commonality. On the following day, July 17, 1429 the Dauphin, Charles VII, was crowned, and anointed by the Holy Church, King of all France. At the head of his entourage was Joan bearing her ensign of Christ above the standards of the other captains of the royal army, for as Joan said:

"It had borne the burden, it was quite right that it receive the honor."

After receiving his coronation Joan kneeling embraced her Sovereign around his legs and crying said:

"Gentle King, now is done God's pleasure, Who willed that I raise the siege of Orléans and that I bring you to this city of Reims to receive your holy sacring, showing that you are true King and him to whom the kingdom of God should belong."

This affectionate scene was the zenith of Joan's life. The glory that was God's to give was bestowed more upon the seventeen year old Commander of the Imperial Forces, who had made this coronation possible, than upon the receiver of the crown. This remarkable era is not remembered in the hearts of the French people because of Charles VII, who proved to be quite unremarkable, but it is remembered and treasured most sacredly because of the spotless and pure Joan, Heroine of France. From all the realm nobles and peasants alike had journeyed to Reims to witness this magnificent event—which fact itself is a testament to the faith the people had in the words of Joan—for Charles himself had feared disappointment up to the day before his crowning. Among those who had so traveled were Jacques d'Arc, Joan's father, and Isabelle, her mother. Can one imagine the tenderness that Joan felt when she saw her beloved parents behold the culminating brilliance of her God-given mission or conceive of that love which she bore those who raised her to be worthy of heavenly revelations? Can one envision the love and esteem of these humble peasants for their little shepherdess exalted to the highest honors and praise that a thankful country could bestow? We strive mightily to visualize this profound drama, but cannot sense a thousandth part of it.

Now it was Joan's desire to march swiftly to Paris to use the momentum the royal army had gained on the road to Reims to full advantage. Had she been allowed to do so the capital city would no doubt have been taken and the Burgundians and English would have lost the war six years earlier than was ultimately the case. But Charles was not a man of action or vision and was easily persuaded to false hopes of diplomatic solutions. Immediately after been crowned king he received emissaries from the Duke of Burgundy who requested a two-week armistice. Joan was excluded from this council. In return for this truce Charles was promised that Paris would be *given* to him without a fight. The Duke of Burgundy had of course not attended the coronation and was still known to be allied to England. Although the Duke had proven himself a treacherous and treasonous enemy yet the gullible new King of France readily accepted his proposition. *His foolishness was a betrayal of Joan and all who had fought so valiantly under her banner.* In truth Burgundy was only brokering for time—for two days earlier, on July 15th, three-thousand five hundred knights had left England bound for Paris. They arrived on July 25th and greatly reinforced the city. Incidentally, Burgundy had been appointed governor of Paris. Had King Charles VII permitted Joan to march on Paris she would have been within the capital walls five days before the arrival of the English reinforcements. As it was, his lack of resolution and his inaction led Joan to express these sentiments:

> "And please God, my Maker, that I may now withdraw myself, leave off arms, and go and serve my father and my mother by keeping the sheep with my sister and my brothers who will rejoice so greatly to see me again."

But this was not to be. The noblemen of the royal blood looked to Joan to continue to lead their army. King Charles seemed impossible to understand. He moved about with his entourage in a seemingly mindless manner from town to town, content with what he had obtained and more in pursuit of his pleasures than in recovering the Kingdom of France. One of his *favorites* was certainly a Burgundian. Completely without Joan's knowledge, the King had entered into negotiations with the enemies of France at a conference in Arras. A Franco-Burgundian truce was signed on August 21, 1429 ironically authorizing the Duke of Burgundy to defend the city of Paris! The last truce had promised that Paris would be given to Charles. Otherwise this truce confirmed the *status quo*, appeasing Charles with the cities Joan had acquired for him and promising a peace conference in Auxerre the following spring. In reality the English and the Burgundians were again simply buying time. Already they were plotting major counter-offensives against France.

Meanwhile, Joan of Arc, the Duke of Alençon and other captains with their men-of-war were finally en-route to Paris. In her *Trial of Condemnation* Joan was asked:

> "When you went up before the town of Paris had you had a revelation from your voices to go there?"

Joan's reply:

> "No, but I went there at the request of noblemen at arms who wanted to make a valiance in arms against Paris and I had every intention to go further and to cross the moats of the town of Paris."

After several skirmishes Joan attacked Paris in force on September 8, 1429. She and the nobles found Paris extremely fortified—in men, in arms, and in war machines. Charles had given his enemies over a month and a half to reinforce the city and prepare its defenses. The battle was fierce and lasted from "noon to about the hour of nightfall." The fighting ceased when Joan was wounded in the thigh by a crossbow bolt. Her men carried her away, and weary themselves from the hours of hard fighting, left the field. The following morning Joan, although seriously injured, rose early and told the Duke of Alençon to sound the trumpets to resume the fray. But the battle for Paris was over. Emissaries from King Charles arrived and commanded that Joan be brought to him. He also had men demolish the bridge over the Seine River to prevent the army's crossing back over to resume the attack. Furthermore, on September 21, 1429 Charles issued an edict that astounded his champions. Pernoud writes:

> "The King gave orders to disband the fine army of the coronation adventure and condemned his war captains to inaction. 'And thus,' wrote de Cagny, 'were the will of the Maid and King's army broken.'"

The naive King Charles felt sure that his court diplomats could achieve more than his royal army and he was confident the planned spring peace conference would restore his kingdom. Why then, he reasoned, should he maintain an army? His stupidity was truly a betrayal and only the hard lessons of experience would teach Charles that liberty is won from foreign oppressors only through great effort and sacrifice. He was to learn that imperialistic tyrants will only listen to diplomats who are backed by military power—and often not even then. Most autocrats will only yield when they have lost in pitched battle. By the time King Charles had learned these essential lessons he had already sacrificed the Maid of Domremy.

Although Charles was deceived, Joan was not. She recovered from her wound and then continued her crusade doing what she could to fight the enemies of her country and prevent the towns she had gained from falling back into Burgundian/English hands. But her resources were very limited as she was not supported by her own Sovereign. In a letter written on November 9, 1429 to the citizens of Riom her great need is clearly demonstrated.

> "Because great quantities of powder, arrows, and other furnishings of war were expended before the [town of Saint-Pierre-le-Moustier] and because the lords who are in this town and I are poorly provided . . . I pray you, as you love the King's

good honor . . . instantly send help . . . of powder, saltpeter, sulfur, arrows, heavy arbalests (missile launchers), and other furnishings of war."

In March of 1430 Joan received word from Reims that they were once again threatened by attack from the Burgundians. She wrote back and promised that she would intervene on their behalf. Joan, with the small army that followed her, did all she could to preserve France. When Joan had arrived at Chinon a year earlier she had said:

"I shall last a year, hardly longer . . . it [is] necessary in that year to toil mightily."

A year had passed, in which she had accomplished her two fold mission, had been wounded at least three times, had been ennobled, and had, through the foolishness and duplicity of Charles, been abandoned. But she would not abandon France. She had lasted the year and still fought on. *It was then she was given a new mission from heaven—one that would be a far greater personal challenge than what she had already endured.* This new task would have sent many a hero or heroine flying to safe haven. It is one thing to be called upon to lead armies to battle. It is quite another thing to rot in the enemy's dungeon. It was revealed to Joan the she would be captured. She testified:

"In Easter week last (April 22, 1430), being upon the moat at Melun, it was told me by the voices of Saint Catherine and Saint Margaret that I should be taken before Saint John's Day, and that so it must be and that I be not dismayed, and take all in good part and that God would help me. . . . I submitted myself above all in the matter of war to the will of the captains, meanwhile however I did not tell them that I had had revelation that I should be taken."

Amazing! She did not question to what purpose her capture would serve. She did not ask relief from God, although she had already undergone tremendous trials and had accomplished with his aid, the miraculous. She did not flee from her pending incarceration. Imprisonment meant suffering, humiliation, torture. She submitted in perfect obedience and thrust herself wholeheartedly into the business of war.

Of course, there was no peace conference between Burgundy and Charles—instead only attacks by the English and the Burgundians upon French cities and towns. On May 6, 1430 Charles VII publicly acknowledged that his adversaries had deceived him. On May 22, 1430 the Burgundians besieged the city of Compiégne. Joan received word that the people there had "resolved to lose their lives, their own, their wives' and their children's" rather than submit. Joan immediately went to their aid, and by night, secretly entered the city. The following day she joined the battle that was raging outside of the city gates. When first she appeared among the ranks of the French the "enemy fell back and was put to flight." Joan charged hard into the Burgundians as was her custom to put herself in the thick of the battle. But as she, and those who followed valiantly after her, became more distant from Compiégne they were ambushed and flanked. The governor of Compiégne saw the surge of the English flank about to enter the bridge, and fearing lest they should enter the city, he ordered the gates of Compiégne closed. Thus Joan and her fellow soldiers were sacrificed to save the town. A Burgundian, George Chastellain relayed these details of Joans capture:

> "The French, with their Maid, were beginning to retreat very slowly, as finding no advantage over their enemies but rather perils and damage. Wherefore the Burgundians, seeing that and being flowing with blood, and not satisfied with having repulsed them in defense . . . struck among them valiantly both afoot and mounted, and did great damage among the French. Of which the Maid, passing the nature of women, took all the brunt, and took great pains to save her company, remaining behind as captain and bravest of her troop. And there Fortune allowed that her glory at last come to an end and that she bear arms no longer;

> "An archer, a rough man and full of spite . . . dragged her to one side by her cloth-of-gold cloak and pulled her from her horse, throwing her flat on the ground; never could she find recourse or succor in her men, try though they might to remount her, but a man of arms called the Bastard of Wandomme, who arrived at the moment of her fall, pressed her so hard that she gave him her faith (surrender) . . . He more joyful than if he had had a King in his hands, took her hastily to Margny, and there held her in his keeping until that day's work was done."

Thus on May 23, 1430 Joan was captured. She was held by John of Luxembourg, first at his camp outside of Compiégne. It was here that that the Duke of Burgundy, ecstatic that at last his mantic Nemesis was ensnared, went to her tent to see for himself this military prodigy. He and his allies made a great "outcry" of "jollity" to see her humbled in captivity. After several days she was taken by Luxembourg to the fortress of Beaulieu-en-Vermandois and then to the castle of Beaurevoir. Her jailers were always men and it seems that the only restraints to their behavior towards Joan were those imposed by Joan herself. The following evidence given under oath by Haimond de Macy, a guard in the service of John of Luxembourg, is an extraordinary testimonial of Joan's continued resolve and her remarkable strength:

> "I saw Joan for the first time when she was shut up in the castle of Beaurevoir for the lord John of Luxembourg. I saw her (many) times in prison and on several occasions conversed with her. I tried several times, playfully, to touch her breasts, trying to put my hand on her chest, the which Joan would not suffer but repulsed me with all her strength. Joan was, indeed, of decent conduct both in speech and act."

Later, at her trial, much was made of her manner of dress. She kept herself attired in man's clothing. The connotation her enemies put upon this action was that she was guilty of unnatural inclination. The truth was nothing of the kind. Her reasons were two fold: first, men's clothing provided her with some measure of defense from molestation, and secondly, although imprisoned she was still a *knight* and would not cease to dress like one without God's permission. She had sat astride a warhorse for over a year and felt that it was imperative to be able to so mount again in a moment's notice. At Beaurevoir she demonstrated the veracity of her motives. Her enemy Macy validated the need to protect her body from her jailers. The latter need she demonstrated herself through two escape attempts. In one of these attempts she was seriously injured when she leaped from a castle tower. When questioned regarding this desperate endeavor she answered simply:

> "The reason why I jumped from the tower was that I had heard that the people in Compiégne, even to children of seven years, were to be put to fire and sword . . . Yet still, my voices forbade me to jump . . .
>
> "I did it, not in despair, but in hope to save my life and to go to the succor of many good people in distress . . .
>
> "I did jump, commending myself to God and Our lady, and I was hurt. And after I had jumped, Saint Catherine's voice told me to be of good cheer and that I would be healed and the people of Compiégne would have succor.

"Afterwards I confessed it, and begged our Lord's pardon for it. And I think it was not right for me to jump—it was wrong."

Why was it wrong for Joan to effect an escape? For the same reason she did not prevent her capture in the first place. Her mission was *now* not to lead the armies of France nor crown the Dauphin. She had awakened the French to their own cause and they must and would continue the battle of independence from England without her. Her mission was now predicated upon her remaining in the hands of her enemies until she died at their hands. Her heaven-sent task was *now* to remain a prisoner. Why was this required of her? These two apparently different callings were actually one. How? What was it that set Joan apart from the other captains of the royal army? First, she was not a fighting captain in the sense that she did not lead her men by the power of her own arm. She did not wield the sword, hacking and thrusting. She rode into the thick of battle as a captain bearing the standard of Christ—literally. Secondly, she did not hearken to the counsel of men—her directives were given her by God and his angels. She testified that He had sent her, that He would enable the French to be victorious, that He was their true Sovereign and that He had selected Charles to be their Ruler under Him. She testified that the English would be defeated and driven from France. She testified of the *how and when* to do battle that would make their triumph possible. She testified that the French people and soldiers had great need of repentance and if they would confess and forsake their sins God would save them. Her testimony inspired the French to action and the result was miraculous. Joan's mission was *now* to testify! An ancient American wrote that the "word had a great tendency to lead the people to do that which was just . . . it had had more powerful effect upon the minds of the people than the sword, or anything else." Joan did not conscript an army. By the power of her "word" she raised and inspired an army. She was a testator! Not only did her own people marvel at her preternatural abilities—so did her enemies.

For the English and Burgundians to recognize that she was sent from the King of Heaven would be an admission of their despotism. Therefore her enemies ascribed her powers to be of Apollyon. It was crucial to them that she be proven a witch. If they could not defeat her on the battlefield they would defeat her under the guise of an ecclesiastic court. Surely, they thought, their predetermined verdict would not only be easily obtained, but their superior legal and clerical minds would easily subordinate an uneducated farm girl still in her teens—thus certifying the intended outcome. However, "God hath chosen the foolish things of the world to confound the wise; and God hath chosen the weak things of the world to confound the things which are mighty." Joan was called to testify—this time to her enemies. Her court testimony would prove to the least enlightened that Joan was of God and that France had been delivered by the Almighty. Were it not for the Trial of Condemnation we would not have the true account of the salvation of the French Nation. Were it not for Joan's witness and others who testified at her trials we would have mostly myth and supposition. Joan's life and her mission were destined to inspire, uplift and benefit all disciples of truth in all ages. Her capture and subsequent trial would be the means of ensuring that such a record was made.

Why was it necessary that Joan suffer death? There are many supposed advantages to bearing false witness but all such vanish in the face of death. To be offered life or death, the balance altered by a word, is the ultimate test of truth. *For the truth, to die; for to live, but lie.* The reason God permitted this young heroine to sacrifice her life demonstrates the vital importance of her mission in the annals of history. She was true to her testimony and sealed it with her own blood.

> "For where a testament [is], there must also of necessity be the death of the testator. For a testament [is] of force after men are dead: otherwise it is of no strength at all while the testator liveth."

Joan was to remain in the custody of John of Luxembourg until November 21, 1430, when she was given into the hands of the English. During these months of imprisonment, competing factions of her enemies vied for the dubious honor of conducting her trial. Church officials were often politically aligned to different secular powers. While the clergy in liberated France regarded Joan as heaven sent, the church hierarchy in Paris and Normandy wanted her condemned as a heretic. The University of Paris petitioned the Duke of Burgundy:

> "Whereas all faithful Christian princes and all other true Catholics are required to extirpate all errors arising against the faith and the scandals which they entail among the simple Christian people . . . We implore you of good affection, you, most puissant prince . . . be sent and brought prisoner to us the said Joan, vehemently suspected of many crimes smacking of heresy, to appear before us and a procurator of the Holy Inquisition."

The Bishop of Beauvias, Pierre Cauchon, wrote:

"It is required by the Bishop of Beauvias . . .[that] the Duke of Burgundy and John of Luxembourg, in the name and on behalf of the King [of England] . . . that the woman who is commonly called Joan the Maid, prisoner, be sent to the King to be delivered over to the Church to hold her trial because she is . . . defamed to have committed many crimes, sortileges (foretelling), idolatry, invocations of enemies (devils) and other cases touching our faith and against that faith."

Joan was a profitable commodity. Representing the King of England, the Bishop offered a ransom of ten thousand francs to Burgundy and to the Bastard of Wandomme, who had captured Joan, a pension of three hundred *livres*. Thus the Duke of Burgundy had custody of Joan, Paris and the King of England wanted Joan. She went to the highest bidder and was sold to the English.

Who was obviously silent in the bidding? Who failed to offer even a token ransom for Joan's life? Charles, King of France! Pernoud writes:

"But need we be surprised? Contemporary accounts of Charles VII agree in showing him to have been of weak character . . ."

"Moreover, it can be seen that the King was very careful to foster his own fame . . . after the recovery of his kingdom he had innumerable medals struck on which he is entitled 'Charles the Victorious.' . . . Once, contrary to all expectation, he had received that crown and sacring which had made him King of France, he was not sorry to see her to whom he owned them put out of the way."

The English took Joan from Beaurevoir to the city of Rouen in Normandy. Normandy had been a fief of the British monarchy for two hundred years. She was incarcerated in the castle of Bouvreil of Rouen on December 23, 1430. On January 9, 1431 Joan's trial commenced. It would end five months later on May 30th. Joan had successfully fought off her Burgundian guards of the previous May through December, for when she was examined in Rouen she was found inviolate. A notary named Boisguillaume testified:

"Joan was examined by some matrons and was found to be a virgin . . . The Duke of Bedford stood in a secret place from which he could see Joan examined."

Although proved a chaste and virtuous maid—remarkable itself in light of the fact that she had been in the company of men for two years, including six months of servitude with male guards, she was derided by her chief judge, the Bishop of Beauvais. Her Jailer, Jean Massieu, provided this account:

> "On several occasions I took Joan from the prison to the place of jurisdiction and passing in front of the castle chapel; at Joan's request I allowed her, in passing, to make her orison (prayer). For this I was reproved by the said Benedict, promoter of the cause, who said to me: 'Truant, who maketh thee so bold to allow that excommunicated whore to approach the church without permission? I will have thee put in a tower so that thou shalt see neither sun nor moon for a month if thou dost so again.'"

The manner in which Joan was questioned is extremely revealing of the duplicity of the trial. Pernoud states:

> "The interrogatories were conducted according to procedures which are still used by examining magistrates. Questions succeed each other without apparent order, some designed to distract the accused's attention, other, reverting suddenly to subjects already explored, intended to lead the accused to contradict [herself]. Joan, without any assistance, kept her end up superbly in the face of these attacks."

Many of the quotations already cited in this work are taken from works citing the account of the Trial of Condemnation. Although the king's secretaries were noted for the omissions and alterations of Joan's testimony, we are indebted to certain notaries who refused to alter the record of Joan's trial that they kept. Such men as Guillaume Manchon scribed records of integrity. It is amazing to see how an unlearned nineteen year old girl defended herself and answered the subtle questions put to her by doctors and clerics.

> Court Interrogator: "Will you leave to the determination of our Holy Mother the Church, all your matters whether in good or in evil?"
>
> Joan: "As for the Church, I love her and would wish to sustain her with all my power for our Christian faith. And it is not I who should be prevented from going to church and hearing mass. As for the good works which I have done . . . I must put my faith in the King of Heaven, who sent me to Charles . . . and you will see that the French will soon win a great thing which God will send . . . I say it [now] that when it happens you may remember that I said it."

Court Interrogator: "Will you abide by the Church's determination for your sayings and deeds?"

Joan: "I abide by God who sent me, by the Holy Virgin and all the saints in paradise. And I am of opinion that it is all one and the same thing, God and the Church, and . . . should make no difficulty. Why do you make difficulty over that?"

Court Interrogator: "There is a Church Triumphant where are God, the Saints, the angels and souls already saved. And there is the Church Militant in which are the Pope, God's vicar on earth, the cardinals and prelates of the Church, the clergy, and all good Christians, and Catholics. This well-composed Church cannot err and is ruled by the Holy Spirit. That is why I ask you whether you are willing to abide by (put your trust in) the Church Militant, that is to say, the one which is on earth, as I have explained to you."

Joan: "I went to the King of France from God and the Virgin Mary and all the saints in paradise and the Church Victorious above and by their commandment. And to that Church I submit all my good deeds and all that I have done and shall do. As for submitting myself to the Church Militant, I shall answer you nothing else for the time being."

Court Interrogator: "Since you say that you wear (a man's) habit by Gods commandment, why do you ask for a woman's shift when it comes to dying?"

Joan: "It will suffice if it be long."

Court Interrogator: "Since you have said that you would wear woman's clothes if you were allowed to go away, would that please God?"

Joan: "I have answered elsewhere that not for anything whatsoever would I take an oath not to put on armor and not to wear man's clothes to do the Lord's commandment."

Court Interrogator: "Do you know whether Saint Catherine and Margaret hate the English?"

Joan: "They love that which God loves and hate that which God hates."

Court Interrogator: "Does God hate the English?"

Joan: "Of the love or hate which God has for the English and of what he does to their souls I know nothing; but well I know that they will be driven out of France, excepting those who will die there, and that God will send victory to the French over the English."

Court Interrogator: "Was God for the English when their cause was prospering in France?"

Joan: "I know not if God hated the French, but I believe that it was His will to let them be stricken for their sins if there were sins among them."

Joan's answer that God allows one nation to inflict suffering upon another in consequence of their transgressions is a tremendous insight into world affairs. It echoes the sentiments of an ancient Israelite who declared that their enemies were a scourge unto his people, to "stir them up in remembrance" of God—and if they would not remember God and heed the scriptures then these enemies would "scourge them even unto destruction." As terrible as war is, the suffering it causes often does awaken a people to their faith. When there is truly none but God to turn to, many do turn to God. Thousands, who have survived the calamities of war, bear witness that it was God who ultimately saved them.

Court Interrogator: "Who was it led you to have painted on your standard angels with arms, feet, legs and clothes?"

Joan: "You have been answered."

Court Interrogator: "Are you going to speak the truth?"

Joan: "You may well ask me some things concerning which I will answer the truth and to another I shall not answer. If you were well informed about me, you ought to wish that I were out of your hands. I have done nothing excepting by revelation. *(Joan turns towards the Bishop)* Consider well what you are about, for in truth I am sent from God, and you are putting yourself in great danger."

Court Interrogator: "Do you know if you are in God's grace?"

Joan: "If I am not, may God bring me to it, if I am, may God keep me in it. I should be the most grieved woman in all the world if I knew myself to be not in the grace of God, and were I in (a state of) sin, I think that the voice would not come to me, and I would that all could hear it as well as I."

Then Joan the Maid becomes Joan the Prophetess:

Joan: "Before seven years be passed, the English will lose a greater gage than they had at Orleans, and they will lose all in France."

Court Interrogator: "How do you know that?"

Joan: "I know it by a revelation which has been made to me, and it will happen before seven years . . . I know it was well as I know that you are there in front of me."

Joan spoke these words in March 1431. The French defeated the English, driving them from Paris, on April 13, 1436.

Court Interrogator: "These saints which appear to you, have they hair?"

Joan: "It is good to know!" (Pernoud's translation: "Wouldn't you just like to know!")

Court Interrogator: "How do they speak?"

Joan: "This voice [of Saint Margaret] is beautiful, sweet and humble and it speaks the French Language."

Court Interrogator: "Does not Saint Margaret speak the English tongue?"

Joan: "How should she speak English since she is not on the side of the English?"

Court Interrogator: "Of what form was Saint Michael when he appeared to you—was he naked?"

Joan: "Do you think God cannot afford to clothe him?"

Court Interrogator: "Had he hair?"

Joan: "Why should it have been cut off?"

Court Interrogator: "What sign did you give the King [the Dauphin] that you were come from God?"

Joan: "I have always told you that you will not drag that out of my mouth. Go ask him!"

Court Interrogator: "Why [were you sent] rather than another?"

Joan: "It pleased God thus to do, by a simple Maid to drive out the King's enemies."

Court Interrogator: "Is there any need for you to confess yourself since you have revelation from your voices that you will be saved?"

Joan: "I believe that one cannot overdo cleansing one's conscience."

Joan always believed that she would be delivered from the power of her enemies. On March 14, 1431 she disclosed that she knew that such deliverance would be through death. She told her interrogator:

"Several times the voices have told me that I should be delivered by great victory. And thereafter my voices say to me: 'Take all in good part, do not whine over thy martyrdom; by it thou shalt come at last to the Kingdom of Paradise.'"

Again and again Joan's captors ordered her to confess heresy and deny her testimony. She knew that if she refused to do so, her judges would murder her. She did not want to die and certainly she pled to God that His will for her might be through a different course. Her mission however, was irrevocable—hence she was told to bear in patience her afflictions and not to complain of her coming death. She was not promised rest in this life. At length the court pronounced her guilty of being a schismatic, an apostate, a liar, a soothsayer, and a blasphemer of God. At this point Joan entered the next stage of her trial which was ironically called "charitable admonitions," for such reprimands as were given the accused in this phase of the proceedings were anything but charitable. It was the procedure to force the accused to admit guilt and suffer penance. Torture was the primary lever used to pry loose confessions. The record continues:

Court Interrogator: "Will you correct and amend yourself according to the decision of the doctors?"

Joan: "Read your book (the record of her trial) and then I will answer you. I trust in God my Creator, in all. I love Him with all my heart . . . you will get nothing else out of me . . . though you were to have my limbs torn off and send the soul out of my body, I should not say otherwise."

On the 24th of May Joan was brought to the cemetery of Saint-Ouen where a scaffold designed to burn her at the stake was being erected. It is one thing to be executed quickly, as in decapitation. It is quite another to be burned alive. After all of her sufferings in prison and her fearless defense in court, Joan was not prepared for the scene which was thus presented to her. She was terribly shaken as she was made to visualize her fiery death-altar. She was lectured, ridiculed, defamed. Her mind was harrowed up by the image of the agony that she would endure as she was slowly consumed in the flames. She was then presented with a cédule of abjuration (a document of renunciation). Her tormentors told her that she must sign or: "this day shalt thou end thy days by fire." The deceitful conduct of her judges at this point approaches the fantastic. According to eye-witnesses, the simple cédule which was read to Joan obligated her to the *least* restraint. It was short—from *five to eight hand-written lines* in length. However, the cédule that was inserted into the official court record was an "artificially fabricated" confession of *forty-seven lines of French type*. This "official" version of the cédule was completely different in content to the cédule that was read to Joan and given her to sign. The actual cédule simply required that she "no longer carry arms nor wear man's clothes, nor shorn hair." In no way did it mandate that Joan deny her revelations. The lengthy fake cédule in the court record has Joan confess that she "feigned lyingly to have had revelations and apparitions from God . . . [of dressing in] clothes dissolute, misshapen and indecent, against natural decency." It further includes confessions of blood lust, blaspheme and apostasy from the Catholic faith. Joan would never have signed such an abjuration.

What of the brief, coarse, handwritten cédule that she did sign? Although Joan had learned to sign her name the English commanded that she endorse the cédule by marking the document a simple cross—as a cross would be easy to forge on the forty-seven line bogus cédule. Of course Joan knew nothing about the counterfeit confession. What is more, when she was told to sign the little cédule that was read to her by marking a cross, Joan laughed! Why? In her days as the commander of the French forces Joan would sometimes send misinformation in her dispatches to deceive the English and Burgundians. Pernoud writes:

"This cross was the sign agreed upon with those of her own side to warn them *not* to believe the contents of a letter."

By marking the cédule with a cross Joan was saying to her followers that she had *not* agreed to even the minor requirements of the document. The horrific tension of the moment was broken. It amused Joan that all she had to do to save her life was place the mark of disavowal upon the cédule. After all she had been through it seemed funny, perhaps ridiculous, to so end her afflictions. However, Joan was soon to learn that even though she signed the cédule with a cross, her own disclaimer, she had displeased God by marking it at all. Although she did not revoke her testimony she had given the appearance of doing so. To this day many believe erroneously that Joan recanted her revelations. Joan testified:

> "My voices have since told me that I did great injury . . . that I had not done well in what I had done.

> "I did not say or mean to revoke my apparitions . . . All I have done I did for fear of the fire and I revoked nothing . . . I would rather make my penitence once and for all, that is to say die, than to suffer any longer the pain of being in prison."

By now Joan realized there was no intent of setting her free. Immediately after she had signed the cédule she was returned to her cell. Her enemies wanted her dead—why then the fiasco of showing her the stake upon which she was to be burned, reading her the document of abjuration, having her place her hand upon it and mark it? The reason is, with all of the expense and effort of the Trial of Condemnation, nothing had been proven against her. Her judges had failed to convincingly convict her of the charges they had levied against her. The real purpose behind the drama her clever judges acted out in the cemetery of Saint-Ouen was to set a snare, lay the foundation for two charges which they would soon bring against her and which could not be denied:

1) That she had returned to the wearing of men's clothes;

2) That she was disobedient to the Holy Church and therefore a heretic.

The first breach of the cédule they ensured by providing her only men's clothing—"her gaolers (jailers) brought none but male attire." But why did she discard her shift to put on these garments? Her enemies gave nothing to chance. Martin Ladvenu stated:

> "A great English Lord entered her prison and tried to take her by force. That was the cause, she said, of her resuming man's clothes."

The second followed the first—her wearing of men's clothing was done in direct opposition to the commandment they gave her not to do so. Thus she proved herself, in the eyes of these corrupt men, guilty of disobedience and therefore a heretic!

On May 28th her "Trial for Relapse" began. This trial would be very brief as only the charges of wearing male attire and disobedience to the church hierarchy needed to be considered.

Court Interrogator: "Have you not made abjuration and promised especially not to resume men's clothes?"

Joan: "I would rather die than remain in irons; but if it be permitted me to go to mass and I be taken to a pleasant prison, and that I have women [jailers] I will be good and will do what the church wishes."

What a sad and heartrending plea! Could any prison be pleasant for a young woman? For Joan, after the ordeal she had endured, yes, if it would not subject her to rape. She only asked that her guards be women, and that she be allowed to worship. Joan promised that if these dignities were given her she would gladly wear a dress and be "good." Her simple request was that she be afforded treatment that was normally given female inmates of ecclesiastical prisons. Nevertheless, the motivation of these wicked men was not to *reform* Joan but to kill her. The church in Rouen was but a puppet of the English Crown. The Bishop of Beauvais knew that if he were to remove Joan from secular incarceration and place her in church confinement that she would keep her word, for it was the first time she had made such a promise. He knew that if she were allowed to do what she said she would do—such a simple matter as wearing women's apparel—it would remove the pretense for her pending execution. Therefore the Bishop refused her petition. He declared her "Heretic, obstinate and relapsed." He left the court and said to his English confederates: "Farewell. It is done."

On the morning of May 30, 1431 a priest by name of Martin Ladvenu came to Joan's cell and administered to her the sacrament of the Lord's Supper. He also explained to Joan that her judges had decreed she was to die that very day by fire. Joan cried with great lamentation, pulling at her hair:

"Alas! Do they treat me thus horribly and cruelly, so that my body, clean and whole, which was never corrupted, must be this day consumed and reduced to ashes! Ah! I had rather seven times be decapitated than to be thus burned. Alas! . . . I appeal before God, the Great Judge, from the great wrongs and grievances being done to me."

Joan was taken to the Old Market Place of Rouen. Her escort included many of the notables from her trial and a company of English men of war, fully armed, numbering "more than eight hundred"—so many men to kill a girl. Beauvais she condemned saying, "Bishop, I die by you." To the others whether they were English, Burgundians, or French, she humbly pardoned and forgave them "the evil they had done her." So powerful was this young woman in these her final moments of her life that many of those whom she absolved wept bitterly. Nicolas Midy preached a final sermon to Joan in the presence of this great company. After he concluded Pierre Cauchon read the irrevocable sentence:

> "We declare that thou, Joan, commonly called the Maid, art fallen into diverse errors and diverse crimes of schism, idolatry, invocation of devils and numerous others . . . And thereafter, after abjuration of thine errors, it is evident that thou hast returned to those same errors and to those crimes, your heart having been beguiled by the author of schism and heresy. . . . Wherefore we declare thee relapsed and heretic."

It was the law then extant that after the ecclesiastical verdict was pronounced that the accused be delivered to secular authority "who alone were qualified to decide the actual sentence and apply it." But the church judges and the civil magistrates were in too much haste to follow legal procedure. Hurriedly she was delivered to *The Master of the Work*, the executioner who "without further ado, seized Joan and took her to the place where the wood was ready." Jean Massieu, an usher, testified of her last moments:

> "When she was abandoned by the Church I was still with her and with great devoutness she asked to have the cross. Hearing that, an Englishman who was present made a little cross of wood from the end of a stick, which he gave her and devoutly she received and kissed it, making pious lamentations to God our Redeemer who had suffered on the Cross, for our redemption. And she put this cross into her bosom, between her flesh and her clothes, and furthermore asked humbly that I enable her to have the cross from the church . . . to hold it raised right before her eyes until the threshold of death."

The Master of the Work was told: "Do Thine Office." Upon hearing this command he set fire to the faggots surrounding the scaffold. As the flames began to scorch and sear her body Joan implored her angels to help her and then she began to cry out in a loud voice:

> "Jesus, Jesus, Jesus, Jesus . . ."

She did not cease calling the name of her Lord until her soul fled to His rest in death.

The sight was too much, even for her tormentors. Master Jean Tressard, secretary to the King of England, wept, and cried in anguish:

"We are all lost, for we have burnt a good and holy person!"

Isambart de la Pierre stated:

"One of the English, a soldier who detested her and who had sworn that with his own hand he would bear a faggot to Joan's pyre, in the moment when he was doing so and heard Joan calling upon the name of Jesus in her last moment, stood stupefied . . . and confessed . . . that he had sinned gravely and that he repented of what he had done against Joan whom he held to be a saintly woman . . ."

Joan's body was reduced to ashes, save her heart, which remained intact. This produced a state of amazement and dread in the executioner who was responsible to see that his open crematorium reduced her body to nothing but dust. Jean Massieu testified that her heart was whole and "full of blood." Isambart said:

"Immediately after the execution, the executioner came to me and my companion Martin Ladvenu, struck and moved to a marvelous repentance and terrible contrition, all in despair, fearing never to obtain pardon . . . for what he had done . . . [for] despite oil, the sulphur and the charcoal which he had applied against Joan's heart, nevertheless he had not by any means been able to consume [it]."

All that was left of the Maid of Domremy spoke in striking symbolism—they could not destroy the courageous heart of the heroine! Isambart further testified:

"And the executioner [said] that he greatly feared to be damned for he had burned a holy woman."

Her death affected the canon of Rouen, Jean Alepée, in a totally different manner. He weeping declared:

"I would that my soul were where I believe this woman's soul to be."

Her ashes and her heart were thrown into the river Seine.

The Old Market Place of Rouen, where Joan was martyred, bears little resemblance today to the public square where the young Maid from the marches of Lorraine suffered unto death. It is too changed to convey to us the spirit of that sad and sacred day when Joan completed her life's mission. One may stand on the banks of the Seine where her charred remains were scattered and feel and hear nothing. The waters are polluted. It is a grave desecrated. Go to Orleans, where a United Kingdom of France was born in the travail of its liberation. There you will find but one whisper from the past. The modern city, with its hundred of thousands, is built on top of the medieval Orleans, cementing the past over in near silence. Along the Rue d'Escures you will find a gallant monument of Joan the Knight upon her white horse—but it inspires without speaking. Yet, if you listen carefully you will hear a murmur that emanates from beneath this statue—for underneath this square, called the Place du Matroi, during a recent excavation, stone archways of Old Orleans were found intact. Beneath *their* span rode the living Joan, astride her war-horse bearing the banner of Christ. No plaque marks the entrance to where these may now been seen, but if you descend some twenty feet below street level you will find a lighted window that unveils their antiquity. It is from these stones you hear sounds nearly inaudible—of the raising of the siege, of the lamentations of the vanquished foes and the exultations of the oppressed made free. We strain to hear and we are not satisfied.

Is there no place where the voice of her great and godly life can reach across the ages and enter into every feeling of the heart? There is one such place, miraculously preserved for more than five hundred years. It is the place of her birth and childhood. Down an unpaved road, little more than a pathway, beyond fields and meadows, is Notre Dame de Bermont, sequestered in the woods. Although its bells are now silent, yet it stands. Be still and you can hear the soft steps of little Jeannette as she runs down the forest path to worship within its chapel walls. Several miles south of Bermont is the village of Domremy nearly untouched by time. The church of Domremy, although enlarged from the one that Joan knew, is still in use to this day. Why did not Joan frequent the Church of Domremy more than the more distant Notre Dame de Bermont? Perhaps she felt more kindly towards the priest of Bermont, or more likely, she could attend mass there many times each week without the harsh scrutiny of her childhood friends who felt her too zealous and devout.

Only a few steps from the Chapel of Domremy stands a small angular shaped house. Its zenith is a half gable, the tallest side of the house plummets straight to the ground from this summit. The structure is two and one-half stories at its height and at the end of the roof's declivity, stands a little over one story. It is built of thick stone and large rough-hewn open beams, the exterior and interior finished with stucco. This highly unusual house is solid and built to stand for a millennia. Four rooms occupy the main floor. The entrance room is the largest—where one is welcomed by a large fireplace, an oversized mantel and a commodious hearth. To the right of this room is another of slightly diminished size. From this second room an open sided staircase leads to the upper chambers. Of the two remaining rooms on the ground floor, one is very small, suitable to serve as a young girl's bedroom. Enter this dwelling with reverence. This is *her* home. It is the home where Jeannette was born, nurtured by her mother, Isabelle, and taught by her father, Jacques. These walls echo with familial sounds, of the laughter of a little girl, of solemn family prayers, and of the sobs of grief stricken parents. Between this home and the church was the garden of Jacques d'Arc where Jeannette received her first revelation. When you stand upon this ground put off your shoes. Here Spirit communes with spirit and you know that Joan's account and testimony are true. A few yards from her front door a clear brook flows quietly down to La Meuse, a stone's throw away. This small river is flanked on either side by lush meadows of grass, green even in February, the month Jeannette last saw its' banks. So vibrant are the colors and so soft the texture of this verdure that it seems to be a painting, artistic strokes from a Master, the oil fresh from the palette—not yet dry. The secret of this effect becomes clear as you walk down into the meadow and discover that a supple carpet of moss is interwoven with the blades of grass. The River Meuse is sufficiently deep here, so that it flows smoothly with only gentle ripples. Hence the light is not refracted over rough stones, for there are none such to disquiet the tranquility of the scene. Rather its waters reflect the cerulean blue of the sky tinted at the borders with celadon mirrored from its embankment.

Look at La Meuse, the nurturer of the child who became an appointed captain of an army, elevated to the rank of general by the men who freely followed her. Look at the river that suckled the savior of France. Oh, how in the Burgundian prison did she long to return and rest by its quiescent waters! Never could she go back to her home or to La Meuse. She could only bid them adieu in her heart and mind. The poet Péguy penned these lines in 1895 while on a pilgrimage to Domremy, written in the first person of Joan d'Arc:

"Farewell, sleep-bringing Meuse and sweet to my childhood
Which remains in the meadow where you run low,
Meuse, farewell, I have torn myself away.

"You will forever flow, a familiar wanderer
In the blessed valley where the green grass grows,
Oh, inexhaustible Meuse, you whom I loved."

Listen to the sound of the pure rolling Meuse and you will hear more than the sound of its mild current. It is the whisperings of three voices, of Michael, Catherine and Margaret. They stir within you the awakening of your own vital purpose, your own life's mission. They say to you that nobody in all the world can do what you have been sent here to do. They tell you not to fear the odds, and to fear, or respect, God, and not man. They say to you, your calling is foreordained. They testify of your divine heritage, that you are a son or daughter of the Almighty. They command you to fight, but not to destroy. They promise that if you lead with the banner of the Lord, victory is assured. They instruct you to uphold others in their rightful positions and to awaken those who are timid to their crowns. In all, they say, give the glory to God and take no honor for your own. They warn you that your way will be difficult and admonish you to be faithful, for by so doing you shall inherit Paradise. They tell you that Jeanette is your sister and that as she endured to the end so can you, despite every opposition of your enemies. Rise to your calling and harken to the voice that declares to you: "Child of God, go, go, go, I shall be at your aid, go!"

Bibliography

Primary Sources

Pernoud, Regine: *Joan of Arc by her Herself and Her Witnesses* (Scarborough House, Lanham, New York, London)

Marot, Pierre: *Joan The Good Lorrainer at Domremy*

Hallam, Henry: *History of Europe During the Middle Ages, Book I: The History of France* (1898 Edition)

Trask, Willard: Joan of Arc *In Her Own Words* (Turtle Point Press, New York)

Ruskin, John: *Harvard Classics, Volume 28*

The Scriptures